Proud and Prejudiced:
a gigolo's tale

For all comments or copyright clearance requests, please contact Mike Harrison at harrisonmike@gmail.com

Acknowledgments
Cover design: Mike Harrison
Guinea Pig (initial read-through): Jeanie Watson
Editing: Mike Harrison and Rich Harris
Dedicated to the memory and inspiration of our friend: Jade Bien-Aimée Sutherland

First edition: February 2008

ISBN 978-0-9556801-0-6

To all the people who thought we wouldn't make it, that'll be £11.99 thanks.

Thursday: My kitchen.

Even though I had been waiting for a call, when the phone finally rang I still jumped slightly. For twenty or so minutes I had been at my stove, mindlessly pushing some broccoli around in a hot pan with not very much else. I may have been a poster boy for healthy living, but I was also the poster boy for unimaginative thinking. Thankful to be distracted from my feeble culinary efforts I answered the call; as I had expected it was Miles. He first sent me a message via my website, making it pointedly clear that he had been lured in by my rather explicit profile picture. Personally I hated resorting to blatant smut but I had to agree with Juan, it really did the job. Miles and I had chatted for the next week or so, just long enough for him to see if I met his requirements – I did, and now he was ready to confirm an appointment. The one thing that stood out about him was that he sounded irate all the time; though it didn't stop me being eager to escort him to a party his firm were throwing at the Hilton. Actually, quite a few of my clients were slightly aggressive by their very nature, but personally I thought that was just a way they covered up the real reason that they wanted to contact me.

Anyone would be wrong in thinking that I casually made my lifestyle choice – not by any stretch of the imagination did they foresee how my sexuality would turn right onto Cock Street. I hadn't actually known I was gay until I was in my early teens and funnily enough, everyone else seemed to be aware of it before I was. I always knew I was different though, that was a given, but I had never quite put a finger on it. Well, not until a cute guy at school put a few fingers on and in it - and I was sold. Unlike the other gay boys at my school who were as flamboyant as one of Liberace's fur-trimmed stage outfits, I didn't really notice any dramatic change in myself. It wasn't until I had left school and started my first job that I realised the potential in my sexual discovery.

I took a part time job at a bank on the high street, which as I predicted turned out to be a drab little building filled with drab little people. Apart from the potted ferns and a girl called Ally, I think I was the only other thing there with an ounce of life. Ally was my only friend there; a big girl who was all mouth, cleavage and curly hair. I only worked with her for a few months, but we really connected, even though I hadn't seen her since. One night she invited me to a party, but really there was a gorgeous guy who was also going and she wanted to add him to her already replete list of conquests - I was the excuse to attend. I was terrified at the thought of it as I never used to party at all and was pretty anxious, nervous and excited about being thrown into a roomful of captive boys. I called her and said I wasn't going but she pleaded with me to come, telling me that she'd look after me. Finally, I had relented and agreed and that night I pulled on my glad rags and combed through my hair. When we arrived I was pleasantly surprised to find it was a pretty mixed event with young and older people crammed into a small and expensive rooftop flat in Chelsea. Ally confided in me (after half a dozen gin & sodas) that she had set her eye on Tom, a smart looking chap who already happened to be in a happy relationship with a stuck-up girl called Amelia. Ally didn't let little details like this put her off though. As the night wore on, she did manage to add him to her list of names, but she also got a cracked rib and a broken finger after Amelia caught them, proving that she wasn't as stuck-up as I had initially thought. As Ally ran past me crying, looking to flee the party with her proverbial tail tucked between her legs, I decided to be a good friend and leave with her, but before I caught up with her I thought about how much of an effort I had gone to – why should I miss out on the fun?

Truth be told it was because there were quite a few fit lads attending the event and I wanted to try my luck with at least one of them. I just hoped that none of them had an Amelia waiting nearby.

As the party carried on I was introduced to a friend of a friend named Juan, who was a gorgeous looking chap; half Latino, half Essex. When I say I was talking to him, it was actually him doing all the talking while I just stared, nothing short of captivated by his gleaming diamond watch that he was no doubt waving before me on purpose, desperate for me to drool all over it. It worked.

"Seventeen hundred pounds, for a watch?" I screeched, doing all I could to stop my jaw hitting the pine-effect flooring with a thud.

Juan kindly explained to me that in his line of work his clients could be very generous, "Especially the old farts" he said with his polished upmarket Essex twang as he laid his hand on my forearm and leant in conspiratorially. "Old shags are the best shags" he declared as if I ought to have known this. He hadn't bothered to spell out the obvious - that he was an escort for men - and I imagined that he probably didn't sit his parents down and tell them he was gay either, he just seemed to be the sort of person who just expected the rest of the world to keep up with his conversation. After the pretty rubbish evening I had endured so far I found him extremely entertaining - I looked on eagerly while he continued.

"They unleash their filthiest fantasies, barely able to fulfil even one of them, blow their load by the time I've touched their zipper and then they hand over great wads of cash."

He went on to tell me how being a gigolo was the best career move he'd ever made. In his finest week to date, he had earned over eleven hundred pounds and in the last three months had been taken to no less than six different countries. I must have looked like a stunned blowfish, as he put a perfectly manicured hand upon my shoulder and told me that if I didn't make an effort to close my mouth, he'd have no option but to stick his dick in it and then charge me £250 for the privilege.

As I was about to ask another thousand questions, he eyed a distinguished-looking gentleman making his way to a buffet table and within a flash he was gone, leaving me blinking repeatedly in a cloud of dissipating Paco Rabanne. Thankfully I'd had the foresight to ask for his number before leaving, and it wasn't long before we chatted again. I knew he was desperate to brag about his work to me, and then it happened - he invited me to go with him on a night's work. I could easily see why he was so popular – he was stunning; mocha coloured skin and a rugby player physique, both rough and pretty all in one with dazzling grey eyes that shone from beneath his perfectly plucked eyebrows, the left one with several lines shaved into it. On his left earlobe sat a chunky, squared diamond and if his watch was anything to go by, it was the real deal.

That evening, as I accompanied him on one of his field trips, I watched from nearby while he sat and laughed with his client, paying attention to his boring conversation, ensuring he was flirting in all the right pregnant pauses. He looked like a master at a fine art gallery opening, showing me it wasn't all about whacking it out and whacking them off. He actually made it look as thought it was the best date he had ever been on.

"Golden rules" he told me afterwards, "make them feel special, flatter them. Laugh if they think they're boring you; smile if they think they're upsetting you. Never yawn. Always listen. Be prepared with conversation topics. Make gentle yet firm, filthy, sexual remarks but don't over step the mark - let them feel in control. That's half the battle won really. Even though you may be tired, not in the mood or would just rather be at home with a glass of wine and some brioche, act like you are simply desperate for them to shove something up you and trust me darling, the money will come just as quickly as they do."

I was surprised at first by how generous he was, letting me in on the inside tricks of his trade, but then again, comparing the two of us, I realised that I would not have been much competition for him anyway.

So, that's how I became a gigolo. From then on it was onwards and upwards. Of course being a gigolo didn't always have to result in sex, thankfully; some of my clients were desperately awful, and as I was my own boss, the whole event was usually under my terms and conditions. I usually had a few restrictions as to what was on the menu, depending on how vile the client was, i.e. no kissing, no rubbing, no wanking, no sucking, no fucking, no licking, no touching and occasionally no eye contact. I neglected to include these restrictions on my personal website and I also neglected to tell them to Miles when we chatted; I'm sure that would have made him sound even more irate.

"Ok, so I will be outside The Hilton at a quarter to. Miles, I'm never late. Ok, bye". Something in his laugh as I ended the call made me feel a tad uneasy, but I put it to the back of my mind – big mistake.

Friday evening: The Hilton, London.

After zipping round the corner and nearly taking out an evening jogger, the silver machine then sped along the road before suddenly roaring to a halt bang outside the hotels entrance, this time almost knocking over one of the doormen. The pretty people who had been waiting in the queue cooed and stretched out their necks, desperate to see who was arriving, seemingly disinterested in the two near attempts of manslaughter from the erratic driving. Even before the car door opened, I knew it would be him.

I hadn't been waiting long – ten, fifteen minutes perhaps. He may have appeared to be an arrogant, chauvinistic arsehole, but at least he was a reasonably punctual one. A very handsome doorman scurried over to the Mercedes and his gloved hand opened the door – I refrained from rolling my eyes at this blatant classist display, instead stepping forward so I could greet him.

Emerging slowly from the cream leather interior, he smirked and dusted down his jacket before glaring right through me, then shot the same disinterested look towards the rest of the people bustling around; obviously he was used to functions like this whereas when I had arrived I couldn't stop myself gawping. I caught his eye and extended my hand, immediately wondering if I was appearing too formal. He didn't take it. As he took a step closer to me, I could immediately smell the whiskey on his breath – probably sunk a good few already I thought to myself. Closely followed on the heels of the whiskey was his aftershave – strong but terribly sexy. Slightly shy of six foot, a generously-liquored Miles now stood before me, all ego and Hugo Boss suit. His jaw was squared and although probably freshly shaved, it still showed off the stain of a five o'clock shadow. Aside from his apparent drink problem and a few inches difference in height he actually looked a little bit like me. He looked me up and down slowly and his eyes stopped when they met mine. An arrogant smile stretched over his face and without saying a word I knew he was the sort of guy who never settled for second best. I returned his gaze without flinching – I wasn't going to let this guy dominate me – I had to do that for another client on Wednesday.

Finally he broke his gaze, looked around and proclaimed to no-one in particular "Gonna be a good night". Giving me the once over again he thoughtfully added, "Definitely, a fucking good night." As soon as he had spoken the words, he strode off towards the entrance, leaving me to chase after him. *Say something!* I thought to myself. "Nice number plate" I cooed, catching up with him as we walked towards the door, one of the doormen looking me up and down as we passed. "Very…apt" I continued, trying to illicit some sort of a response from him. He didn't respond - he simply grabbed my arse as I walked in with him, making me jump with surprise. Feeling slightly uneasy, I glanced over my shoulder to see a doorman jetting off in Miles' shiny car. Before it sped away I caught a last glimpse of the registration plate. "PL4Y I30Y indeed" I mumbled to myself – a serious sense of foreboding washed over me.

Inside one of the ballrooms, waiters slid around with trays of bubbling flutes and delicious looking treats, each barely big enough to get stuck in between your teeth, while a backdrop of flamboyant chatter filled the room. Everyone was dressed to thrill; ladies with perfect cleavages, micro minis and sky high stilettos; people-shaped advertising spaces for the very latest of the fashion elite and the entire room exuded the aroma of money. The oddest couples danced around us; elderly gentlemen with gaggles of tiny blond girls in their wakes; fat, middle aged women covered in furs and dripping with diamonds coupled with ridiculously beautiful young men at their side. The old dears reminded me of a drag party I went to some years ago, but the sparkle here was top quality, not the tacky stuff that I bought online.

We were ushered to our VIP booth and immediately given a magnum of Champagne by the host - apparently, one never needed to approve a bottle of Bollinger before it was opened. Two glasses were poured and set down before us. I still wasn't feeling totally confident, even though I had been to a couple of functions like this – I could just never really let it all go to my head – it all seemed terribly pretentious and as I was only there for the money, it really was a bit fake. I was much more relaxed when having a few pints at my local with friends as we shared a selection of crisps, also known as a buffet dinner.

Miles reached out and picked up a glass which I stupidly presumed he was going to hand to me. I'd barely moved my hand to take it when he guzzled the lot in one gulp. Setting the glass down, he grimaced and faced me. "Fucking Bollinger? I told them Dom! Don't they fucking listen?" Then he raised his voice and repeated "DON'T THEY FUCKING LISTEN?" I flushed with colour. Luckily the waiters were much too gracious to show any offence and carried about their business as usual. I bit my lip and decided not to tell Miles he was being a prat.

After a few dirty comments from Miles and a few awkward silences from myself, I realised I should commence my well rehearsed routine, but before I could even utter any of my repertoire, two men bearing drinks came rushing over. They both looked incredibly red in the face and highly intoxicated so I tried not to take too much notice of them, instead reaching for my champagne. The two gentlemen (although judging from their dishevelled appearance I'm sure they left that title behind five or six drinks ago) plonked themselves opposite us in the booth, never letting go of their drinks, nor pausing in their conversation to introduce themselves. From the moment I was aware of them they had been wrapped up in bubbly conversation, stopping only to include Miles or to swig from their drinks. I gathered they were business colleagues of Miles and from their conversation I managed to pick out the following: tonight's party was invariably mediocre and was nowhere near as grand as the Hyatt soiree several years prior; tomorrow Miles was expected to turn up for golf no later than lunchtime; and that the thinner, balding newcomer one on the left was "definitely on" with Miriam, the new receptionist with the massive tits: lucky Miriam.

Time to pour myself more champers. Miles had just topped himself up for this third glass, so I only had to do the honours for myself. I reached over and pulled the bottle out as carefully as I could, I wasn't sure I could afford to break anything in this place, drinks included. As I poured, the conversation fell to a hush and when I looked up all eyes were on me. I felt a little embarrassed and exposed but tried to remain calm and in control, spilling only a splash or two of Bolly on the table.

"Jeremy Trent, Vice President of Hudson Gamble & Trent Enterprises. Enjoying the party?"

"Oh hello, nice to meet you" I said, putting the bottle back in the cooler and taking a generous swig of my drink. "Rich Harrison, friend of Miles. And yes, it's a really nice party". Faker than a Fendi for a fiver, I mused.

Jeremy seemed to sweep past my opinion, and with disbelief repeated loudly "Friend of Miles? Miles doesn't have any friends" to which all three men burst out in laughter.

I faked a smile. "Oh, yes very funny". The third gentleman looking somewhat serious reached across the table and patted his sweaty hand on mine.

"If I may give you a word of advice young man, I'd watch this one" and he nodded his head in Miles' direction. "Not so much an eye for the ladies" he continued "but an eye for their fella's as well!" His bulging eyes hung on Miles and simultaneously the three men erupted into laughter once more.

For the next half hour I endured the most torturous conversation full of in-jokes, office gossip and middle-aged fantasy. Fortunately our host was terribly attentive and the champagne flowed freely. At one stage I opened my mouth to join in, but nothing came out. I was simply going through the motions of joviality. Jeremy piped up again.

"Last year at the Marriott – um, have you been to the Marriott?" he spoke so quickly I wasn't able to respond, but I sensed he didn't really care "this one disappears for over forty-five minutes" he said with his eyes wide, thumbing at Miles. "So, me and old Marcus here, decided to go and seek him out – forgot our brandies though, didn't we?"

"Brandies, yes" Marcus repeated suddenly looking very staid.

"So we toddled along to every room but where was Miles?" his eyes seemed to grow even larger and I was starting to get concerned for him – my first aid certificate had lapsed in the late nineties.

"We don't need to hear this old rubbish" Miles threw in. "Old news, boring!"

"So," Jeremy continued "after hunting in every bloody room, we ended up in the car park, God only knows how come."

"Car park!" exclaimed Marcus, his eyes widening a little and the start of a smile teasing the corners of his mouth.

"And then we spied the Merc!" Jeremy proclaimed in a very Poirot kind of way. By this point I was desperate to reach for my drink again but felt it would be inappropriate to interrupt, so I carried on sitting there with a daft look on my face, listening with intent.

"The windows were all steamed up!" Jeremy proclaimed. "So we sneaky-sneaky up to the bloody thing and rap on the window". Marcus was now creased up in silent laughter. Miles, who was furrowing his brow slightly, was swirling around the dregs of his drink and Jeremy was looking delighted with himself, a man on the verge of culminating a truly epic story.

"So we knocked on the window and shouted 'Oi Hudson, you randy old devil, who's the tart?' And the window rolled down and inside…inside was Miles, and the bloody chauffer!"

"Chauffer!" Marcus echoed, slamming his fist down on the table.

This time no laughter came. Silence hung in the air for a painful moment. Jeremy looked at me, his eyes encouraging me to comprehend his scandalous story. Luckily I was the boy scout of the escorting world and was prepared for anything so I picked up my glass, took a long slug and leant forward with my response.

"I once blew a doorman at a club some years ago. I was desperate to get in but wasn't on the guest list and you know what arseholes these doormen can be. So, after a bit of, lets call it *persuasive talking*, I ended up in the back seat of his car." I wiggled my little finger and continued. "Tiny little winkle! I could have used it to floss with! Mind you, bloody good club though – didn't get home 'til three the next morning" I ended with a smile.

Miles looked at me and shook his head, Jeremy slumped back in his seat with a look of horror on his face and Marcus veered his body to the far right and vomited in the corner of the booth.

All that could be heard was the near-silent hum of the cars engine as we sped down Regent Street. It was nearly 2am, the party was still pumping away, but given the night's events, it had been best to make an early exit. Neither of us spoke, what was there to talk about? Thankfully, we were under the control of a very capable chauffer – Miles was much too plastered to even get in the car, let alone drive it. I caught the chauffeur's eye in the rear view mirror and my mind jolted back to that tedious story about Miles. How could I have been so stupid? Why did I have to go one better? I generally drank only one or two to lubricate conversation and relax around new clients. Unfortunately, in the short time I had laboured over the three Stooges' conversation, I had drunk three quarters of a bottle of champagne. Once I'd had a few, my resourcefulness and more importantly, my skill of keeping my tongue in check went out the window.

It would seem that my story did nothing to please any of my party guests; otherwise Jeremy wouldn't have got up and stormed away to the bar. And had he not done that, I doubt very much he would have tripped over Miles' Chief Accountant and given himself a concussion from head-butting the bar, needing then to be whisked away to the nearest hospital. It's also safe to assume that this unpleasantness is what caused Miles to down his drink like it was going out of fashion and I can only imagine that he forgot he was on double Jacks all night which made him pick up whichever drink was nearest to try and dampen the fire in his throat. Unfortunately, big-titted Miriam, who was standing near the booth, and her Sambuka did little to soothe his senses. Honestly, I'd never seen anyone vomit so ferociously.

Rather than assisting my client who would have by this time been sprawled on the floor of the bathroom, I decided to finish off the Bolly and molest the buffet tables. Well, what other chances would I get to indulge in such style? Eventually I checked on him, and seeing the wreck he had transformed himself into, swiftly called upon the host to find us a chauffer. Upon passing the booth on the way out with Miles propped against me, I noticed a new bottle of Bolly being placed into an ice bucket. Ever the economist and hating waste I swiped it and stashed it under my arm.

"Window" Miles bleated desperately, bringing my attention back to the present. I reached over and pressed the button. As the window vanished, a stream of cool air and night time noise instantly filled the car.

"I like you" Miles said weakly, smiling a crooked drunk smile as his eyes rolled back into his head.

"Oh, well, I like you too!" I responded with feigned politeness as I chugged back the last of the champagne, having been the receiver of too many drunken pledges of affection. If my friends could see me now, they'd be so proud.

"No not *you*. I like *you*! I like your silliness" and then he giggled. Whatever could he mean? "When we get back to my place, I'm going to take you to heaven."

Oh god, there was no way I could handle any more of this night. "Miles, that's really very sweet, but I'm in no mood to go clubbing – I'm quite tired actually".

"More silliness" he declared loudly, punching his fist into the air as if making a point. "Not *Heaven* clubbing *Heaven*, but heaven!" he gestured to his groin and managed a pathetic pelvic thrust, then began slurring about how he was going to flip me over and do all sorts of filthy things to me, but inwardly I sighed. I decided not to linger on this and turned to the window, gazing out on a beautifully illuminated London.

I woke up with a start, sensing I was not in my own bedroom. The enormous and luxurious bed underneath me confirmed my moment of panic. No, I was still at his. With a very present headache I vowed never to drink again. It was actually rather stupid of me to get so drunk while working, but not much point in crying over drunken champagne now. I tried to push myself up, but my hands sunk deep into the plush mattress, offering me no support whatsoever. Immediately I took in the wonderful décor of his bedroom, something that no man alone could ever conjure up on his own, and certainly not a man like Miles. He more than likely had a team of decorators and interior designers in – the poor saps, they probably had to put up with his groping and a barrage of sexually derogative remarks as they tried to roller and stipple along quietly. I let my head fall back into the silk pillow, and found myself staring at my own reflection in the huge mirror on the ceiling. It was quite surreal to see myself floating up there, like some kind of horrific out of body experience that I couldn't stop. It was then that I realised Miles was still next to me. The bed was so big he must have been a foot or more away, but there he was, all wrapped up in the covers like an expensive rice-paper roll. I thought about waking him but decided against it. Given the state he was in last night, he could do with the extra sleep.

On the bedside table next to me I saw my watch and my ring sitting on a copy of 'Easy Home Stencilling'. I shook my head and continued looking; two un-opened condoms, two empty bottles of poppers – that explained my headache at least. I looked all around for a clock but couldn't see one, and noticing the sun shining brightly outside, I was actually thankful that it had woken me. Freeing myself from my expensive fabric prison I swung my legs over the side of the bed and jumped down delicately to find I was naked, save for a sock. The rest of my clothes were bundled up on the floor at the foot of the bed. Quickly, I stepped into my boxer shorts thankful to have something on finally, but as I tried to pull on the other sock, I bumped the bed, waking Miles.

"Err, morning". I blurted out, not knowing what else to say.

He sat bolt upright, probably still half drunk, looking at me with squinted eyes and interest. When it finally registered with him who I was and why I was there, he laid back down.

"Erm, sorry Miles – where's the loo?" I added.

"The en-suite's being re-decorated. Out the room, turn right, fourth door along."

I shut the door behind me, pausing a moment with my back resting on it, inhaling deeply. As I stood in the upstairs hallway I took in the sheer size of his house – it was like a giant maze – corridors left and right with doors galore. Fourth door along, I couldn't even see where door number one was. If I'd have known I'd have arranged a taxi and a small day bag.

Arriving at the end of the corridor and turning a corner, I found the fourth door. Upon opening it and peering in, I gasped in delight and threw the door wide open. The bathroom was exquisite, just like something out of 'OK! Magazine'. In fact, I could almost have pictured Miles laying in the sunken bath in the middle of the room, sipping at a glass of champagne; the caption would've probably read 'Fucking Bollinger?'

As I gazed around I saw all the mod cons one would expect in a glamorous room like this; LCD TV in the wall, fireplace, Jacuzzi – far too good a room to take a dump in. I was overwhelmed and didn't know what to play with first. I looked into the tub longingly wishing I could have filled it up and dived into the bubbles. Then I remembered where I was and regained my composure. After I had washed my hands and smoothed on some lovely hand lotion I decided to head back, get dressed and leave. On the landing outside I turned to walk back to his bedroom but stopped mid-stride. If it was as late as I thought, then I would really need to get cracking – I had a ton of stuff to get done. I decided to quickly seek out a clock, just to get me back on track. I did a one-eighty and ventured on past the opulent bathroom, and after a couple of standard but terribly large bedrooms furnished with four-posters and Middle Eastern furniture, the next room was sure to be of help: the study.

I bounded into the room. "Oh yes, very nice, very, very nice. I bet none of this is flat-pack!" The room that spanned out before me was amazing, making me feel like I had just stepped into the future; a glass and chrome metropolis. This room was perfect; clean, clinical yet welcoming. An undressed window gave way to a harsh sunlight that bounced off every shiny surface. As I neared the glass-covered work station, furnished with 22" paper-thin monitor and keyboard, my reflection glared up at me. To the right of the monitor was the rare object of the house.

"Ah, thank fuck, a clock!"

5:48am blinked innocently. Was that all? It had seemed so much later. With a few hours still in my favour, I cheekily decided to quickly check my email – that way I could knock down my list of things to do and free up some time. I pulled out the hefty leather chair in front of the desk with a grunt and sat my naked self down. The initial touch of the leather cushioning my vulnerability was cold, but within a minute or two I was warming up nicely. I looked down at the plush carpet, noticing the damaging dents the chair had made.

"Lets see" I said with glee, my hands eagerly spreading out over the desk, assuming the first position of the computer ballet. My right hand reached out for the wireless mouse and I gave it a little shake. The monitor sprang to life and I could hear a tiny hum of the electricity surging into the screen, a most welcoming sound. Some people needed a cigarette or two to get the most out of them in the morning; others preferred a liquidised concoction of fruit and vegetables to get their endorphins screaming. I simply needed a wireless modem and an internet account.

I double-clicked to open a browser with the initial idea of seeing what saucy websites Miles had saved into his favourites before thinking better of it. I didn't have to wait long, this wasn't my cranky old laptop, and this was state of the art hi-speed broadband. The first thing I actually did was load up my homepage to check my next appointments. Seeing there were too many messages and appointments for me to sift through, I moved on to my email account, thinking Juan would appreciate a quick email from me giving him my night's rundown. Before I could even type, a dark blue bar floating at the bottom of the screen flashed impatiently. I was being Instant Messaged. Knowing it was wrong I still clicked to bring up the chat window.

DAVID: Hey hey!

Wow! David was hot, although he probably thought I was Miles.

DAVID: Hey, click accept dude, I've got a BIG surprise for you!

Well – it would've been rude not to at least have a look. As soon as I clicked 'Accept', I was viewing a live feed of David's big surprise. And it was big. And it wasn't that much of a surprise. For a moment all I could do was stare. Instantly I reached down and grabbed my own big surprise.

DAVID: u like? When we meeting up? Am free this afternoon if u r.

I thought about trying to squeeze another client out of this internet rendezvous, but then I realised that if he thought I was Miles, he would more than likely charge me. I decided to ignore him, slipped off my boxer shorts and carried on enjoying his performance.

DAVID: cat got ur tongue?

MILES: Sorry – was just busy. Can't meet today, soz.

DAVID: It's ok, I can see that ur busy. Mind standing up so I can get a better view then mr?

Panic suddenly hit me like a tidal wave. There must have been a webcam in the room. Standing up I looked around.

DAVID: oh yes, THAT'S wot I talking about. Give it 2 me u horny stud.

As I sat back down, I noticed the camera lens was part of the monitor, no bigger than a ten pence piece, but definitely a camera. Just then, David began to do something with a large plastic implement that totally made me lose my concentration. I watched, mesmerised as he put on a one-man show. He was clearly very gifted in this department and I should've said something but all I could do was to keep up a steady rhythm of my own as I gawped at the screen. Within a matter of minutes I was ready to finish myself off when I suddenly remembered I wasn't at home. Several thoughts ran through my head at amazing speed:

a) It was very wrong to be naked in someone else's study;
b) It was also very wrong to be jacking off to some stranger who thought I was someone else;
c) It was probably wrong for me to jizz all over this lovely desk.

I did the only thing I could and cupped my hand as the climax broke, feeling the relief as I bucked my hips. Gingerly, I typed a polite thank you message to David with my clean hand when I heard the cough come floating in over my shoulder. Reluctantly I turned around and attempted a disarming smile, standing up quickly. Realising I was still semi hard with my boxer shorts around my ankles; I covered myself but forgetting what I had just done, did myself and the carpet a disservice. My eyes met Miles' and I was beyond embarrassed.

"Morning Miles. Lovely study."

Tuesday.

I spent most of Sunday in bed, trying to sleep off the shame of a hideous Saturday. After Miles asked me to leave, I treated myself to a taxi home with my earnings and crawled into bed. I had dithered over whether or not to call for the fifth time and explain, but I felt it best to let sleeping dogs lie. The fact that he wasn't picking up any of my previous calls, nor returning my long-winded and pointless voicemail messages, had no influence on this decision. After a good night's sleep, I decided that it would be much more sensible for me to plough on and start servicing the rest of the male population in London. Thankfully, I had many more clients I could alienate and harass before I ended up at Social Services.

It was 4pm on Monday afternoon and I was hanging out some washing when my phone rang. Catching it on the third ring, I found myself talking to Sean from Finsbury Park. He sounded very nice and told me that he got my number through one of my other clients who recently moved up to Manchester. Clearly my name was being bantered around up north. Sean's strong northern accent was riddled with mischief – a weakness of mine. He had very recently moved to North London, within the last week, and wanted me to escort him out to a club on Thursday night to sample the nightlife down south. He didn't have a job yet, so partying on a school night wasn't an issue for either of us. He went on to explain that most of his friends were back in Manchester where he had been living for some years and he was just really gagging for a night out in London. Part of me wondered why he didn't just go out on his own, but then I remembered how scary it was for me when I first went out alone. Soho wasn't the most innocent of places so I sympathised with him and we made our plans to meet up, of course after discussing my fee.

Thursday night; waiting for Sean.

Considering he was twenty minutes late, I felt like I'd been put into the very predicament I would never want to be in. I had tried acting cool and suave since I'd arrived, sidling up to the bar with a swagger, instantly taking up a position among the bustle, trying to look like I owned the place. However, given that every person had taken half a second to look me up and down since I had walked in (and not given me further attention), my confidence had started to falter.

I ordered a drink and glanced around, peering over the rim of the glass to see if anyone was looking at me. God, I felt so awkward! Were they even looking at me? I felt very odd sitting in a bar in London all alone; like one of those odd guys who my friends and I now made fun of. I knew I looked silly sitting there, frantically gulping at my drink and finishing it in minutes. The barman probably thought I was some old alcoholic so I instantly ordered another one and tried to calm myself while I waited for Sean. He was getting later and later and I was feeling more and more awkward. I decided to get up and have a wander, although it didn't make me feel any more comfortable so I looked for a seat until I found a table with no-one at it and practically ran over, making sure no-one got there first. My canter across the floor was rewarded with a perfect vacancy in the corner, looking out at everyone. Better yet, the table was situated in good perving distance toward the toilet door. I wasn't sure how much eye flirting you could do with someone who was busting for a pee, but I was in the prime position to give it a go.

I finally started to calm a little, thinking up ways to keep myself occupied and take my thoughts off the eyes that are watching me. I took my phone from my pocket to pretend I was waiting for a call – that made me feel a little less obvious. Just as I was calming down, a young guy walked over to me.

"This space is taken?" the little Chinese boy asked, referring to the tiny gap between myself and the other patrons.

"No, all yours" I replied, trying to be friendly and smiling at him. Ok, my bad judgment – he wasn't a boy – he was about forty, but he had great skin.

"You have drink?" he said though his smile. I responded by holding up my glass.

"Yes, thank you". I thought it best to be curt; I didn't want to lead him on.

"My name Tran, your name?" he asked, still smiling.

I had to say I was feeling a little flattered and ordinarily would probably have taken the time to sit and chat with him, but as I was working and Sean was bound to arrive at any moment, I had to be cruel to be kind in my own way – this being to pretend I was just in the middle of a call and that he had interrupted me. I put my mobile to my ear and started speaking.

"Sorry, can you just hold a second, thanks." I pulled the phone from my ear and covered the mouthpiece. "I'm sorry Tran – this is a very important business call and I really can't chat, but have a great night" I said trying my best to look apologetic. He looked a little saddened, but as I put the phone back to my ear to finish my business call, the bloody thing started to ring and flash. It was Sean. I put a finger in my ear and yelled into the mouthpiece, realising that because people were now turning to look at me, then it probably wasn't as loud in there as I had first assumed.

Sean spent the first minute of the phone call apologising profusely, saying that he was at the hospital with his aunt. He was lodging with her at her flat until he found a place of his own and apparently she had gotten one of her Ugg boots caught in the top step of the stairs that afternoon and went for a headfirst visit to the downstairs landing. He apologised again saying that he wasn't allowed to have a mobile phone turned on in the waiting room and he was now calling me from outside. Thankfully Aunt Bee wasn't dead, though I hope she felt bad for making me wait by myself. He went on to say that he probably wouldn't be able to leave her unattended for a week or so, but if I wanted to meet up another night and maybe come over for a drink, it wouldn't be a problem. The thought of a grown man lodging with his aunt was bad enough – the thought of a grown man with an escort in the room next to the aunt with a broken leg was somewhat problematic. I knew I should have been more direct with him, but I didn't like the thought of hurting someone's feelings, so instead of saying outright "No", I said "Well, that would be lovely, thank you".

We arranged to meet at Finsbury Park station next Thursday at 7pm, and as I was about to hang up, I realised that I didn't even know what he looked like. He said he was young-looking, with light-coloured hair, blue eyes and about six foot. Conjuring up images of Jason Donovan and Leonardo DiCaprio, I dribbled into the phone and foolishly trusted this interpretation.

As planned, I disembarked the Jubilee line a few minutes before 7pm and as I made my way to the exit I hoped this was going to be a better evening. Clearly things hadn't started out so well with Sean given that he had a relation who'd been admitted to hospital last time we tried to meet up – but then again, perhaps clumsy instances like that were a beautiful beginning to great partnerships in life...oh, I shouldn't think of it as a partnership, I should treat this as a strict business transaction, like; Sean makes a deposit into my account shortly after I make one in him. Funny, must remember to tell that one to Jacqui and Debs next time we go for a drink – they'd appreciate it.

As I waited outside the station entrance, I found myself blatantly eyeing up every guy that walked past in the vain hope that they were him. I checked my watch again - twenty five minutes late. Not a good start really when you consider he kept me waiting last week and I'm missing Big Brother for this. Maybe Aunt Bee has had a stroke?

It suddenly dawned on me that there were two entrances to this station; I figured he was waiting at the other end so I followed the road round and took a good look. Horrified, I spotted him among a few people, taking a stab in the dark that it was him; I doubted very much he was a toddler, a pregnant lady, or a Yorkshire terrier. The old man in the grey cardigan and beige slacks must have been him. When he turned to face me I wanted to run, but my feet felt tacked to the pavement. It must have be the disbelief that made me stare for so long. Sean was looking very pleased with himself; he must have thought all of his Christmases had come at once.

"Rich?"

"Sean!" I replied, somewhat overly enthusiastically, striding up to him and shaking his hand with both of mine, cursing my feet for now suddenly deciding to move. "Hi, how are you? I didn't realise there were two entrances to the station, I'd been waiting around the other side for ages. I thought you weren't going to show." Why was I rambling on so much and why was I giving him the impression I would simply die if he didn't strip me naked and ravish me then and there?

"I wasn't sure you'd show actually, but I'm glad you did." He cooed.

Without waiting for me to respond he was directing me to a bus stop, stupidly under the impression I was going to go home with him. Over his shoulder, I could see a pub, glowing like an oasis in a desert to a hot and thirsty man. From the quick glance I had, it also appeared to be the crustiest looking pub I had ever seen, however I couldn't have gotten there quick enough - anything to avoid going back to his Aunt's.

"Oh, that place looks great! Hey, since you've walked all the way down here we may as well go for a cheeky pint or two." I grinned and forcefully changed his direction with a well-timed grab to the top of his arm.

"Oh…well…if you want" he said, obviously disappointed we weren't on the way back to his bedroom for God-knew-what.

I threw open the door to the pub enthusiastically, giving the impression that I had this pub on my list of *101 things to do before I died*. Inside it was pretty much how I expected it to look; dark, dank and dreary. For a Thursday evening it was surprisingly busy – actually, for a squalid shit-hole it was surprisingly busy. I ordered us a round of drinks at the bar and motioned to a booth in the corner, suggesting we should chat for a while to get to know each other and hopefully long enough for me to think of an exit strategy and get the fuck out of there, I added to my thoughts.

As I sipped at my lager, I looked over the rim of my glass to chance a proper look at him while he fidgeted with his cardigan. Sean, who just told me he was 32, looked like he'd had a very hard life. His face was creased just about everywhere - even the creases had creases. His eyes peered out from their sunken sockets like two black stones and the grey cardigan he wore did nothing at all for him; it was actually hard to see where the cardigan ended and he began. But it wasn't just his appearance that was solemn; as we chatted, he managed to depress me beyond any measure. Generally, I was quite a happy-go-lucky person with a positive outlook on life, but after fifteen minutes with Sean, I was just about ready to top myself. If I had to pick one of his main flaws, (I'd be hard pushed to whittle it down to ten), but it would be that he kept going on about how he was single and that no one would ever want to date him. Without sounding heartless, I wasn't fucking surprised.

"So, you've just moved to London? That must be exciting for you" I exclaimed suddenly, hopeful that the statement was relevant to what he was crapping on about.

"It's only a room in my aunt's place, nothing to get too excited about." He peered at me with his head slightly lowered; his eyes lacked any spark of life and his cheeks were sunken little pits on his face. He looked tired, slightly crazy and I was a little un-nerved.

"Right — but just think" I continued enthusiastically "that's your room. I imagine you'll probably want to decorate it…?

"I was going to do it blue…."

"Blue — great, blue is good. You strike me as a blue kind of guy" I said, obviously meaning it a little more literally than it came across.

He sat for a moment, finished picking the label off his beer, deposited the shreds inside the now-empty bottle and carried on talking. "It doesn't matter what colour I paint it, does it? No one's going to see it but me. No one wants me". Alarm bells were sounding in my head. Oh, it was just the poker machine next to me. I wondered if I would be out of line if I threw my beer over him, closely followed by a good hard slap. Then it might make him snap out of it.

"I'm sure that's not true, you've got loads going for you!" I offered, although, I couldn't think of any right then.

"We should drink up and go. We can catch a bus and get to mine before nine. My aunt doesn't like to be disturbed too late." Hearing this I ran to the bar for another round of drinks, and he swiftly carried on depressing the life from me. About twenty minutes later, he stood and began fastening his cardigan. I heaved a sigh and followed him out onto the high street like a prisoner condemned to death being taken to the gallows.

"Come on then, let's get you back home. Do you have enough fare money? It's not far anyway."

"You know what, it's been a really great night, but I'm shattered – let's call it a night and I'll call you in the week to meet up again?" I said cheerily, my smile belying my urgent desperation to get the hell away from him.

He stopped a minute, contemplating my suggestion. Looking at his watch, he furrowed his brow and then looked back at me. "Nah, come on, we'll go now. We can still catch my aunt if we're lucky".

Yes, that would make us lucky wouldn't it, all three of us having a nice cosy chat about the lack of cock in his life over a nice slice of ginger cake. God, what if she was just as bad as him. I imagined the two of them, together on the sofa, woeful and downtrodden, bawling into each other's lonely arms while I looked on, sipping my tea.

Sean walked towards the bus stop and I could do little else but follow, even though I tried to walk as slowly as I could, fumbling in my pocket in the vain hope that I had left my travel pass at home. I hadn't. I had to do something – there was no way on this earth I was going back with him. I could see tomorrow's new headlines already after they found my body stuffed into some wall cavity, his Aunt quoted in big bold letters "He was a quiet boy, kept himself to himself mostly."

"Sean, sorry mate, it's no good, I have to go, I'm just really tired." I said, putting a yawn on the last few words – desperate times call for desperate measures. I think I can finally understand why someone would gnaw their arm off if caught in a trap.

He stopped in his tracks, just a foot or so from the busy bus stop. "I knew it" he said dramatically. "Why don't you just say it outright, go on. Tell me you don't fancy me." He stood there looking at me, waiting for a reply. Out of the corner of my eye, I noticed a couple of heads turn in our direction – it seemed this conversation was a little more enticing than a wait for the bus. I quickly had to think of what to say in response but try to convey tact and diplomacy, but still get across that yes, he was right, I didn't fancy him.

"It's not that, I'm just tired – I was up early and I didn't sleep too well …"

"Say it – you don't fancy me."

"Sean" I said quietly, "let's discuss this somewhere else, hmm?" Another couple of heads turned.

Before he could speak another word he tilted his head to one side. I watched as it contorted, his eyes going squinty. Oh my God – he was about to bloody cry!

"You…don't…fancy…me, do you?" he began to blub through his tears.

"I er, well, shhh, let's go and talk about…shhh…"

"You…don't…fancy…ME!!" he finished with a shout. By this point everyone at the bus stop and some people strolling on the other side of the street stopped to watch this fabulous spectacle.

Oh sweet Jesus, was this really happening to me? Sadly it was, but the only thing that was in my favour was that the bus pulled up. Most of my audience, hesitant though they were, boarded the bus and left us standing alone. My relief was quickly replaced by slight panic. He was obviously emotionally unstable; I'd read about all the nutters out there. I could be standing in front of one of them as we spoke. I had to keep calm – I didn't want to upset him. Well, not any more that I already had. Clearly the tired route wasn't working – time to try something a little different.

"Now Sean, come on, let's be adult about this" I said, offering him a quick pat on the shoulder. "I'm sorry, I don't fancy you – but you know what – who knows what is around the corner for any of us? Just because I don't, you could meet your Mr Right in the next ten minutes! I'm not going to lie to you, say I like you and lead you on; that's not fair. You just have to realise that sometimes, the people we like don't always feel the same way about us. That doesn't mean I don't like you – you're a great guy – you've got so much going for you! You've got your room, you've got...you know, you've got the room, and it will be blue soon. Wow. So many things! Chin up eh!" I said through a pantomime smile. I just wished, like in any good panto, I could've shouted *behind you* and ran off while his back was turned.

Well, it may actually have worked. He stopped crying. Unless it was the calm before the storm, Perhaps he was waiting for his eyes to dry so that when he cleavered me through the head with a machete, he would've been able to aim better.

"So, we're friends though?" he sniffed. It was time for my finale.

"Yeah, we're friends. Friends, is what we definitely are, we are two...friends."

"So, will you call me in the week for that drink and stuff?" He looked so sad, like a little tyke on the first day of school. How could I have refused? All too easily, but I wasn't going to let on to him!

"Yes. Yes I will. I have your number, and when I get home I know just what I'm going to do with it!" *D-E-L-E-T-E.* "I'll store it in my mobile and we'll go out, being friends."

I had never been so happy to be on public transport in London as I was on the bus ride home – I nearly kissed the driver as the bus sped me away from Sean who was left standing at the bus stop.

Sainsbury's – Fulham Broadway.

I know some people found relaxation in supermarket shopping, but they couldn't be normal. I supposed it was a time for them to draw away and switch off from the stress of their lives, while they meandered around the shop wondering what to pluck from the shelves for tea.

Not for me. I hated grocery shopping with a passion. When people saw me in the supermarket, it must have been like waving a red rag to a bull - they would single me out from everyone else. Old ladies would bash their trolleys into mine, small children would whiz past me, sending my basket into a spin, and more often than not, I would break something expensive.

However, today was to be a shopping trip like many before, but with one special buy that I wouldn't be able to turn down.

My list had been clipped to the top of my trolley: the more organised I was at the start, the less shopping time I would have to endure. Although I hated shopping for groceries, I did love cooking. I was generally quite good at it, but have had a few incidences.

Last Christmas, I received a very expensive set of pots and pans – the type made of cast iron. A few days after I had received them, I tried to make a tuna steak with black bean salsa – though I had given up, exhausted, with one shrivelled up piece of tuna, two singed fingers and one cracked ceramic floor tile after dropping the saucepan when discovering that handles get hot too.

My friends Jacqui and Debs recently bought me a large and swanky cook book for my birthday and I decided to treat them to a thank-you meal by cooking something from it; it was with the best intentions that I welcomed them in for some home-made canapés and polite conversation as I feverishly worked away in the kitchen, occasionally shouting out some additions to the conversation. I decided to have a quick break and a chat to the girls properly after I had dished out the entrées. It was only when we were on our second bottle of wine that Debs noticed the orange glow from the kitchen, which prompted my memory of the brandy-poached fish, still on the stove top. Quick-thinking Jacqui tried to smother the flame with a tea-towel but only succeeded in moving the fire from one side of the kitchen to the other as she screamed and threw the burning cloth. Since then, given the nervous nature of my friends when I suggest any future dinner parties, I tended not to get much opportunity to improve on my culinary skills.

As I was meandering up and down the fresh produce aisle, my saucer-like eyes didn't know what to take in first. Everything looked so tempting and fresh. I wanted to buy it all but I really wouldn't have known what to do with some lady's fingers and a pomelo if my life had depended on it, so I stuck to the reliable tomatoes and carrots. Out into the grocery aisles, I stood before a plethora of tins and boxes with inviting pictures and names, but had to stick to my list where I could. Of course, I'd just been down the aisle with the crisps, sweets and small baked goods so had already filled my trolley with random shiny packets of sugar.

As I pushed my trolley around into the next aisle, I conducted a quick re-cap of my list to see if I'd missed anything, but then I saw him - Mr Incredible; just hanging out down the detergents aisle. Now that was what I called a special offer; he was gorgeous and was bending down to pick up a box of washing powder from the bottom shelf revealing the waistband of his D&Gs from inside his loose-fitting jeans. Just then I decided that I actually loved shopping and made a mental vow to come every day. Obviously, stunning men like this didn't come along every few minutes, so I would have to seize the moment. What's that clever Latin phrase that was really apt – oh yes, 'Carpe Arsey'. Gosh I was funny. I had two choices; I could approach him, compliment him on his fine choice of underwear and loose-fitting jeans, making flirty small talk and bagging his phone number, or I could be a real sad git and hide by the cream crackers and just stare. As I took my place among the water biscuits, I continued my perve-fest from a safe distance. All was going well until he scooted out of aisle seven and disappeared around into household goods. I decided to follow him.

As I moved off I glanced into my trolley. Shit, the entire top layer of my groceries must have had a combined calorie count of infinity. I needed to have a trolley tidy up - after all, one could tell a lot about someone just by looking in their trolley. From what I saw of his basket, the overflowing greenness of the fresh vegetables told me he was fit, super healthy and in prime condition. Glancing trolley-wards, mine said that I had tooth cavities, a spare tyre around my waist and the mental age of a nine year old. Pushing the bags of fun-sized chocolate bars and the fresh in-store baked tarts to one side, I desperately tried to pluck the healthier items to the top. These consisted of two boxes of cereal bars; chocolate flavoured; six-pints of milk, chocolate flavoured and three tomatoes. There wasn't enough health there to hide everything, so as a desperate measure I pulled my pack of toilet paper to place on top. I probably shouldn't really have bought the bulk buy twelve-pack though. I mean he would probably think it was my hobby or something. "What do you do for fun?" "Oh you know, sit on the toilet all day long – I have twelve rolls after all". I wish I had grabbed more fresh fruit and veg; at least then he'd know that I enjoyed cooking. Maybe I could raise that point after saying hello? Maybe I was reading into this too much?

I moved on to household goods and saw him at the end, walking off. He was fast and I needed to speed. He only had a small basket but I was pushing my own bodyweight in baked goods in a trolley that didn't run straight. As I broke into a half run, the wheels wobbled all over the place and I almost hit a display of tragic seventies films that hade been converted to DVD. For a fleeting moment as I hurtled down aisle 7, my mind started to wander. Perhaps it was due to the sheer stupidity of me running through Sainsbury's, chasing a man I didn't know, with a sweet-laden trolley, but I thought that if a book was ever to be written about desperate men in desperate circumstances, my escapade would certainly feature as a whole chapter of its own. I was never like this: when I first got into the gigolo business, I had offers all over the place, and I'm not talking bad ones either. These were from guys that were good looking, great in bed and weren't freaks. Of course, until recently I hadn't been interested in finding anyone for a relationship; I wanted to play the field and earn some cash, I mean, I had always been the child who stayed out too long at recess while everyone else went back in to class. Now it seemed that all the available guys in London had been bagged back in the late nineties – and the ones that remained were freaks, psychos or nutjobs. Taking into consideration that the chance of seeing someone half decent was remote at best, on this rare occasion was it so wrong to pursue something with him? Pursue maybe - chase down with a trolley, maybe not.

I was at the end of aisle 7 now, and had made excellent time, I was sure he was just around the corner, I just needed a quick turn and……………….FUCK!!!!! The in-store cleaner had been tending to a spill and I skidded right into the warning cone - as if that was going to stop someone who was hurtling along at 20mph toward the check-outs. I lost my balance, my legs slid out from under me at an angle until I was jack-knifing along. Several terrified shoppers ran for cover as I screamed like a siren. I really should have let go of my trolley but fear had stopped my hands from working. Suddenly one of the wheels on my trolley locked and the whole bloody thing turned on its side, sending various items hurtling across the floor. I was slowing, but not quickly enough and I ploughed head-long into an end-of-aisle display of chocolate Hobnobs. As the multitude of biscuit packets finally came to a rest, I looked around me. Typical of the British populous, everyone had gathered around me, but no one offered to help at all.

"That's right, just stand there and stare, that's really helpful!" I shouted to no one in particular. Regardless of my comment everyone continued to watch bug-eyed as I picked up my now squashed box of Mr Kipling's from the mess and attempted to regain some amount of composure. I could feel the blood rushing to my head as I started to turn a deep shade of crimson. I felt a bit like a school kid that had just been busted for shoplifting. People were whispering and muttering.

While I repositioned myself onto my hands and knees to retrieve the groceries in the chocolate rubble, I realised that I had landed bottom-first on a pack of biscuits and my fawn-coloured trousers were now heavily stained. Great, I had completely embarrassed myself in front of everyone in Sainsbury's and it now appeared that I had shat myself, bloody perfect.

I didn't know what to pick up first; the cardboard shelving, the several hundred packets of Hobnobs or the calorie-laced items of my trolley that were now so spread out around me that I might as well have just pinned them to my clothing. I was close to tears through shame and the injustice of it all, but before I had a chance to indulge in self-pity, I heard a voice from above me.

"Excuse me…yours, I believe"

I looked up and there in front of my face was the twelve-pack of toilet paper. Oh God, please don't let it be…!

"Oh, um…thanks." I said feebly, taking the toilet paper, knowing my face was about to burst into flames. The hottest guy in the world was looking at me, but I couldn't bring myself to make eye contact with him. "You know, buying bulk certainly is the way to go. I mean it's not like I enjoy buying such a large packet of…of…"

My voice faltered as I plucked up the courage to look my mystery man in the eyes. Oh, he was perfect. Usually from afar, guys I lusted after looked fantastic – it was when I got closer that it all came undone. I was running in the park last summer when a cute guy headed towards me on rollerblades. From a distance, I swore I was looking at Adam Rickett, however, as he passed me, he looked more like Anne Widdecombe.

I smiled politely as I got up, the packet of toilet paper still in my grip. I brushed down my trousers with my free hand, serving only to wipe chocolate from my backside to my hands. He smiled back at me, showing a row of perfectly white teeth; his cheeky grin made me melt, just like the chocolate all over my rear end. *Say something, you idiot,* the voice in my head shouted at me. I was desperately looking around for something to talk about, but my mouth had gone dry. I was about to offer to take him for a drink as a thank you, but as soon as I opened my mouth to brave the question, I was rudely interrupted by a loud, piercing voice.

"Dylan – are you coming?" I looked over to the checkout, where a middle-aged man was casting his eyes between my new husband and me. He had a derisive smirk on his face as he looked me up and down. I looked down at myself, seeing the chocolate all over my trousers.

"Glad you're okay. Maybe next time you'll let me drive – at least then you won't lose your Nair." I glanced down to where he looking and saw the tube of hair remover I had picked up on the way in. Oh…my…God, could this have gotten any more embarrassing? Dylan smiled at me as he turned and wandered back to the cash register. I couldn't take my eyes off him, but someone was standing next to me, talking. Dylan's body was amazing, even through loose-fitting jeans and polo shirt; I could see what was on offer. I wondered who that other guy was, maybe it was his father? Oh…fathers don't touch their children like that - well some do, but they usually ended up in jail. I couldn't believe it; my perfect man surely wasn't dating that old crusty bastard? I came back to my senses and realised that it was the store manager who was talking to me, well, berating really. I paid for my toilet paper (all the rest of my produce was damaged beyond belief) and left. I didn't care who saw me now – it felt like I was in love.

Yo Sushi! Harvey Nicks, Top Floor.

After a quick spot of morning shopping on Tottenham Court Road, I had called Juan to meet up for lunch. He told me that he was able to squeeze me in for a power lunch between a couple of his appointments. As I was waiting for him, I was lost in a train of thought. It had been three days since my shopping fiasco, and three days of being literally besotted by some cute guy who I nearly ran down with a speeding trolley. So far I had used half of a toilet roll.

"Ciao darling" Juan sang out to me from the top of the escalator and brought me back to the present. You could always tell when he was in the vicinity as there was a certain air of expectation around. It was almost like waiting for Barbra Streisand to come blowing out onto stage. He glided past the restaurant hosts, waving them away with a flick of his manicured hand as they tried to talk to him, and sauntered over to me, throwing two air kisses my way and sitting down at the bench. Then he popped open a pocket mirror and started to preen himself, launching into a story about his last appointment's erection problems, catching the attention of over half the patrons around the square sushi train; Juan did not do conversation by halves.

I couldn't help but look him up and down as he shared with me the more intimate details of his client's issues. He was dressed in open-toe snakeskin mules, tight pinstripe trousers and a completely see-through, button-down shirt which is covered in a garish floral design. On anyone else it would have looked ridiculous, but typical Juan – it looked fabulous. He usually only ever did up one button on his shirt, apparently missing the whole point of clothing, leaving his tightly toned chest and abs visible at all times as advertising material. Personally, I never really had advertising materials for what I had was ruined by beer and crisps long ago. His hair was slicked back into a small ponytail and he was wearing gigantic D&G sunglasses that seemed to envelop half his head. He was one of those people who was so flamboyant and over the top, yet he was never seen as camp or effeminate. Blessed with dark olive skin and a rich accent, most people simply put it down to the eccentricities of the British Latino set. To say he was a chameleon was an understatement. One day I would meet him and he would be dressed in a fitted tracksuit with designer stubble and David Beckham-inspired bling. The next it would be in a three-piece, hand-made Italian suit with diamond cufflinks and two-hundred pound Chelsea boots. This new ensemble was for his 3 o'clock appointment, 'Special K'; one of his older clients, although I have never found out why he was called that. The one time I asked, he was so distracted by someone walking past, I was ignored. I had learned that when it came to conversing with Juan, you just let him speak – if you needed to pose a question, it usually had to relate to him or else be asked in the company of extremely ugly people so he remained focused.

"Right" he said with finality, snapping shut his mirror, obviously now happy with his appearance and completely unaware of the shocked looks from our fellow patrons who just had to hear, in loud volume, how he had to shove a dildo up his client's arse last night just to get him aroused.

He looked me up and down and I could tell that I hadn't met his standards by the look he gave me – it was almost pity, or what he could muster up that resembled pity.

"Rich, what's wrong with you?" he asked, as he grabbed some sashimi that was passing him by on the sushi train.

"Oh…nothing…it's all cool", I ventured, putting on a brave smile. Most normal people would have seen through my response and prompted me to go on and explain how I couldn't stop thinking of a guy I didn't even know. Juan, however, started telling me about one of his other clients that he serviced just the other weekend; a rich Canadian playboy who was in his mid-thirties and didn't know what he wanted with his life. Great, give me a few more years and that would be me, save the fact I wasn't Canadian. Nor did I have three million pounds. Or a yacht.

I looked at him while he was telling me, in embarrassing volume and intimate detail, exactly what he and the Canadian got up to on the weekend. My stomach lurched as I looked over to see an elderly couple sharing a plate of tempura prawns; both were looking over at us, chopsticks half-way to their gaping mouths, frozen like a Geiger sculpture in mid scream. I met the old woman's eyes and gave her a pleading look, trying to convey that yes, I agreed, discussing the difference between dental dams and just ramming your tongue up someone's backside probably wasn't suitable lunchtime conversation for Harvey Nicholls. The elderly couple thankfully found their rhythm and got on with their meal, probably discussing the two delinquents sitting across the sushi train from them. I found myself staring at them while Juan went on about his gymnastic floor-fucking routine. My heart sank as I stared at them, knowing I would probably never have that in my life; a life-long marriage to someone who I was utterly devoted to, someone who I could talk easily with, even after being together for decades. I always thought that old people ran out of things to say when they turned forty and spent the twilight of their years taking turns running each other down to the local club to play bingo. Maybe that was more romantic than I thought.

I turned back to Juan who had thankfully climaxed (for the second time) in his story and was now looking expectantly at me, waiting for my praise and adulation at his craftsmanship. Really, you'd think that he'd just shown me a Turner seascape he whipped up last night. I gave him his due and asked a few questions to let him know that I was indeed listening. After 14 plates of sushi and perhaps a few too many sakes, I found myself queuing up behind the old couple to pay for lunch. As we stepped up to pay, I watched them stroll off into the exotic jams and preserves aisle in the grocery section, still talking and holding hands.

I opened my wallet to pay, but with a 'tch tch' from Juan and a wag of his finger, he charged it to his black Amex. The cashier recognised the significance of the card's status and fawned over him, hoping to extract a fat tip. Typical to the economist that he was, he struck out the tip line on the receipt with as much disdain as if he were striking out the cashier from history. As his pen slid over the till receipt in very non-descript and steady cursive writing, I watched him form his signature – Charles Cooper.

He took the card and with a "right then", pulled me out of the restaurant and towards the elevator. He must have noticed my quizzical expression because before I had the chance to ask, he tapped me on the nose with the card and beamed at me. "This is what we, in the industry, call a perk."

Health Clinic, Kensington.

People don't usually like to talk about their work out of the office as it was boring and encroached on their personal time, quite understandable if you worked in an office all day, five days a week. That wasn't quite the same in the sex industry though. All you needed to do was mention something construed as remotely sexual to Juan, and he would tell you, in minute detail, about his last lewd adventure, although he was always careful not to use people's real names, thereby protecting their privacy. I tended to roll my eyes whenever he reminded me of this. I figured that most people used fake names when they booked an appointment with me anyway. I seriously doubted that I had actually slept with Dallas Falcon, Robert-Ray de Marco and Khrys Royale in the last fortnight. Unlike Juan, I found talking about sex a little embarrassing, especially when it was with a doctor, as I could always sense their underlying judgement when they asked me about my past and I answered with "Gay", "Yes" and "I've lost count".

HIV and Hepatitis tests should really be much simpler (and quicker), considering that every second charity event is raising money to combat these viruses. I think making people line up in a doctor's surgery for an hour, then having to wait for weeks for a result is a clever ploy to put people off sex altogether. Thankfully, the waiting room I was currently sat in was practically deserted. It was those times that I was thankful I chose my own working hours. The only other people waiting were a short, balding man with over-sized reading glasses and a mother with her three children, all of which were under the age of five. Two of the brats were playing tug-of-war with a battered version of a Miffy book; the third was in its pram, staring at me. I never understood why infants stared at me all the time. It was as if they have some sort of heightened awareness to my uncomfortable state and they fed off it. I wasn't paternal by any measure, but I smiled down at it, trying to placate it and get it to look somewhere else when the mother looked up from her magazine and with an audible tut, moved the pram to her other side. I went back to my severely out-dated `House & Garden` magazine, thankful it was no longer able to stare at me. It was hazardous for single, grown men like me to be around children because every mother probably assumed that we were perverts who wanted to corrupt their child. Sometimes I wished that I had more balls. Any of my friends would've gone off at them with some diatribe of how they were overreacting and should actually be happy that society was interacting with their child. I felt sorry for the children – they were probably going to be wrapped up in cotton wool for the rest of......

"*Mr* Harrison" said the woman behind the counter very snottily, obviously for the second, possibly the third time.

"Oh, um...yes – thank you. Sorry" I stammered, putting down my magazine and walking over to the counter.

"Second door on the right" she said, looking me up and down as if forming her own diagnosis as to why I was there, apparent mental problems, judging from the look on her face.

"Thank you" I said to her again as she stared right through me.

I walked into the empty doctor's office and took a seat, having a nosey look around the room while I was alone. Doctors really don't seem to make much of a home at their work. A few years ago, during a slow period of escorting, I took a temp job in an office to supplement my earnings, and I'd heard that making yourself a little home in the office adds to job satisfaction and increased productivity. To ensure I felt totally comfy, I completely covered my desk area with erroneous knick-knacks and memorabilia from my past – possibly too much memorabilia, given I was fired two days later because of my 'Dieux du Stades' French Rugby League calendar, matching coffee mug, screensaver and mouse mat. Though I still maintain that if you can't see a cock, it's not offensive.

I wondered what was keeping Dr Finlay, I thought, as I noticed the name plate on the desk. I wondered if Dr Finlay was actually a he, and if he was cute. Every doctor I'd ever had in my life had been either a dirty old man or someone terribly gifted from the Middle East and I usually had no idea what he was saying. Don't get me wrong, I'm not being racist, it's just that I have a terrible ear for accents. I usually just smiled and nodded. Regrettably, last time I did that I ended up with a tetanus booster shot in my arse and I couldn't feel anything for a week which wasn't helpful when you were in my line of work. Surely, given my luck in the past - the odds were in favour for him being nice this time around.

"Sorry about the wait, Mr Harrison" sounds a smooth voice from behind me. From my right hand side, Dr Finlay came into vision – all six foot three of him. Yes he was a man – and what a man! Hello, Doctor! It seemed lady luck had finally arrived.

He looked to be in his early thirties and was stunning; modern, yet professional, haircut, part African American; his skin was smooth and dark and his eyes were an intense green. Framing his beautiful eyes were square glasses, most likely Prada judging from the almost-invisible white stripe running through them. His outfit was progressive but respectful of his position; light whiskered jeans, checked tight cowboy shirt and brown blazer - Abercrombie meets Gant. I wasn't sure if it was just me, but I thought that in the few seconds since he'd spoken, he had been assessing me as well.

"Hi there, no prob" I smiled, trying to be cool and nonchalant. Juan always says that the way to get a man to want you is to play it down, way down. Apparently I had an approach that was too eager. The last time I really liked a guy, I had a restraining order served against me; well, was it my fault that his answering machine cut off my messages half way through and I had to call back? Was it my fault that I had to leave eleven messages just to ask him what he was doing for bloody dinner?

"So Rich, you've come in for a few tests today. Usually we get the nurse to do these, but she's away today and as you're the only one, I'll be doing them for you" he informed me as he took his seat behind his desk and looked at me. I wasn't actually sure if it was nice to be thankful for someone to be sick, but I needed to buy this nurse some flowers for not being here today. Oh, I should say something.

"Yes – you know, just thought I'd check myself out. I know I'll be okay, you know – what with protection and all that. Yes I'm very safe as I think it's very important, especially nowadays with all the young people running around…"

Play it cool you idiot, my conscious shouted in my ear.

"I mean…whatever, I've got some time to kill".

Nice one my conscious said. *It looks like you've got nothing else in your life other than sitting in a doctor's surgery.*

I smiled at him, hoping to undo the lunacy I'd already displayed. Oh, why am I not Juan?

"I wouldn't expect you to be referring to other people as young" smiled Dr Finlay at me, turning slightly in his chair to wiggle the mouse on his computer to take his screen off power-saver mode. "I need to ask you a few questions before I take your blood. Don't worry" he added, noticing me shift in my chair a little "they're routine questions, nothing too taxing for you".

"Oh…that's fine" I said, looking down as I smiled, giving him my best Princess Diana demure, but alluring look. It was then that I realised I was wearing the most hideous outfit. I had been out the night before and didn't get home until after 2am. When the alarm went off this morning just before 9, I just threw on whatever was closet with the thought of going back home after my appointment for a shower and a late breakfast. I tried as best I could to smooth my Marks and Spencer's jumper down and tucked my loafer-clad feet under my chair so he wouldn't notice them. Thankfully all I could find were my Guess jeans that are very snug around the crotch and showed off my arse immeasurably. I must remember to write to *Guess* and thank them.

"Right, can you tell me your full name please?" he said, moving his eyes from the monitor to me. God, they're so beautiful behind those glasses.

"Oh, right – um… sorry. Yes okay – it's Richard" I smiled.

Dr Finlay was about to say something when I interrupted him "Oh FULL name – like all my names, not the long version of my first name? It's Richard Harrison".

I felt my face burn red and this wasn't even the hard bit. He was going to ask me what I did for a living, but maybe not though. I mean it wasn't as if it had any bearing on a sexual disease – I was sure he'd just go on to ask me how many partners I'd had. Crap - that would be even worse.

"Profession?"

Shit!

"Oh… well I am a… professional entertainer" I said, stumbling over myself, not even bothering to think of what I was saying. "You know those people you call up when you are going to a party and maybe you want them to come over and be with you, or tell you a few jokes, or tie some balloons together. Well I mean, I can't actually tie balloons together, nor am I good at telling jokes… although I guess I CAN be funny. Mostly it's not really a conscious thing, especially when I'm nervous or if I like someone. I suppose I just keep talking… like now… and people usually find that funny… I guess." My voice trailed off and I coughed politely.

"So, are you um – an escort?" he ventured, completely calm and without judgement.

"Well, if you want to be concise about it, yes" I said, still not game to look back up. I was sure he knew that my face was about to burst into flames. I don't think anyone had ever really understood me when I was this nervous before, yet he was reading me loud and clear.

"Okay great. Now - how many partners have you been with this year?"

Oh God, oh God, oh God, I can't do this - I wanted an ugly doctor again.

"Um…is there a limit? Do you have checkboxes – like 0-10, 10-20…..20 plus?" I said, not even knowing where to begin counting. I made eye contact with him and he smiled at me. Was that a pity smile or was he suppressing a fit of laughter?

"We can do it that way if you like Richard." Oh God I nearly creamed my pants – he called me Richard.

"20 plus" I said, looking back down to my jeans.

"Would you say you were gay, bi or straight?" he asked, moving his eyes back to the monitor, probably sensing that if he were to make eye contact with me, I'd pass out from the terror of the questioning.

"Gay" I said with surprising firmness. After dealing with the trauma of coming out of the closet and being alienated and disowned by most of my family and apparent friends, this was one thing that I was sure of and something that I had to deal with all on my own.

"Okay great" said Dr Finlay, typing away on the keyboard. Was that a smile that just crept onto his face? I think this may actually be okay.

"Last one – do you practice safe sex?" he said this time looking me dead in the eye.

"Do I practice safe sex? If you're talking about carrying around pepper spray for all the freaks I come across, yeah I'm looking into it."

Surprisingly, Dr Finlay laughed out loud and slapped the table with his hand. I supposed he could empathise with the dating scene out there, but I didn't know if he was Arthur or Martha. Hey, why couldn't I ask him the same questions?

"But yes, I always use a condom when conducting in sex" I said methodically, quoting my Year 10 sex-ed teacher. Of course she was talking about a man and a woman having sex in the missionary position. If I could tell her what I had experienced since leaving school she'd drop dead on the spot.

"Good to hear" said Dr Finlay. He typed a few more things into the computer and then reached into his set of drawers. Out on the desk he placed a box of latex gloves, a few empty vials, some antiseptic fluid, a rubber strap and a syringe. It made me quietly laugh to myself as I thought how similar this process was when I watched Juan getting ready for a night out.

He came around to my side of the desk and with a slightly husky voice asked "Can you take your jumper off please?" He coughed, trying to clear his throat, could it be he was as nervous as I was?

I swallowed hard as I pulled my jumper over my head, roughing up my hair as I did, imagining that it most likely looked as hideous as the rest of me. One saving grace was that I had on a black and well-fitted FCUK t-shirt. He smiled down at me as he sat on the edge of the desk between my spread legs. He tied the rubber strap around my bicep (thankful for the gym visit yesterday) and held my forearm while he rubbed the antiseptic on the inside of my elbow. His fingers moved ever so slightly over my skin, sending it into little shivers of delight. Oh God…no. I felt the blood rushing into my groin and I closed my eyes. I couldn't bone up in front of a hot doctor — I tried to think un-sexy thoughts. I was thinking of my old headmistress, of sumo wrestlers, of Delia Smith rubbing extra virgin olive-oil over herself whilst writhing around on her bench top. It wasn't working.

"You don't need to close your eyes, it won't hurt that much" he reassured me. I opened them and found myself staring right into his, completely mesmerised as he guided the needle in. The blood started to stream into the first attached vial. Surprisingly, he let one hand trace lightly down my forearm and into my hand where it stayed for a few seconds. I could just imagine the giant ripping sound that was about to issue forth from my crotch as I burst through the lining of my jeans. While he was changing vials and putting the full one on the desk behind him, I tried to reposition myself with my free hand while his head was turned. He turned back and his eyes flicked down to me as I was adjusting myself. *Oh God, someone kill me please*, I wailed in my head. He looked back to me and smiled, and then looked back to the vial. I used this chance to quickly look at his body. It was hard to tell what sort of shape he was in while he was wearing his jacket, although I could tell from the veins in his hands and wrists that he must've worked out. That and his shoulders seemed to be straining at the jacket as he was leaning over me. A third vial was inserted and he glanced at my crotch again. "Don't worry, it happens to me quite a bit" he said.

"Sorry" I immediately gushed. "I don't usually get hard-ons in strange doctors' offices" I said, smiling sheepishly.

His brow furrowed and he shot me a puzzled expression for a few seconds, and then added "I was referring to the blood I spilled from the vial. I was saying that it happens to me a bit as I tend to let the nurses do this sort of thing".

Oh my God, what is wrong with me? Please let this be over now, now, now.

After a few more excruciating moments where nothing was said, he finished taking the blood, pulled out the syringe and put a cotton ball over the vein and motioned for me to hold it in place. He walked back around his desk and wrote on some labels, then attached them to my vials. I put my jumper back on, waiting for the all-clear to get the hell out of there. He looked up at me and, for the first time since coming in, looked very serious.

"Now, Mr Harrison, Richard…"

"Please, Rich is fine" I interrupted.

Dr Finlay nodded and continued, "Rich, this may be a very inappropriate question and feel free to tell me that I'm out of line, but I was wondering if...I could persuade you to come over to mine one night. You know, to tie some balloons together and tell some jokes?"

I was about to remind him that I couldn't actually tie balloons, but then I realised he didn't want me to. I was being propositioned. *Oh, dirty doctor* I thought to myself. Before I could say yes, I instantly got an image of the guy from the supermarket and for some peculiar reason I half-thought about telling him where to stick his proposal. But then I remembered - I didn't even know who this guy from the shop was, let alone know if I'd ever see him again. I needed people like Dr Finlay to ensure I got paid, and people like Dr Finlay needed people like me to ensure they got laid.

I wrote down my number and left it with him, and as I walked out of his office, I made sure I clenched my buttocks to enhance their pertness. Letting out a laugh of disbelief in the waiting room, I winked at the nurse who had scorned toward me. Perhaps my bumbling stupidity attracted some people. I glanced back over my shoulder at the nurse once again who was flipping me the middle finger behind my back. Ok, not everyone.

Sainsbury's – Fulham Broadway. Again.

I had been walking up and down aisle seven for over an hour. I didn't need anything from this aisle. In fact, I didn't really need any shopping. I was only there in case Mr Incredible came back. So, I had taken to loitering in supermarkets. Furthermore, I had dollied myself up a little, just in case. Haircut, freshly shaved, nothing that could really be misconstrued as going out of my way though. As for the suit, well, maybe he wouldn't even notice. I was feeling a bit conspicuous as there was a security guard who was keeping an eye on me, and it could only have been for one of three reasons:

Reason one – he wanted me; he wanted me and he felt the need to do me in every conceivable way possible;

Reason two – he thought I was a crazed shopper about to make a break for the display of oven-ready chickens, running off into the sunset like a madman with a penchant for good, easy home cooking; or

Reason three – he had recognised me from past career in television. Well, I say career, maybe that wasn't the best word for it.

Many years ago, a friend and I decided to apply for free tickets to be part of a studio audience on some second rate chat show. It was one of those American-style talk shows, but with very British guests. We arrived at the studio and took our seats a row or two from the front, it was all very exciting. We wondered what the topic of the show would be, as they generally revealed that on the day of filming. It turned out today's segment was 'My Love-Rat Boyfriend slept with my Brother'. My friend and I cooed with delight as we heard this and couldn't wait for filming to begin.

A mediocre warm-up guy tried to whip the audience up and get us engaged for the main act. Trouble was he was so hopeless, that everyone just chatted through the whole of his segment. When he went offstage, our host, Terry, was welcomed on. Terry was offered some polite applause by the lukewarm audience. Terry brushed down his acrylic suit and took his seat under all the lights, soon welcoming the first guest to the stage. In walked a lovely looking lady named Michelle, who took a seat to explain her story. Michelle told us how she had met Scott while they were at school together and had been dating for several years. The show's producers had obviously tried to Americanise it up and spice it up a little, so Michelle from Leeds had been perma-tanned, had a huge mop of over-teased hair on her head and was chewing away on gum and kept referring to Scott as 'her man'. After a while, Scott came bounding onto the stage; a slight of a man who couldn't possibly weigh more than 8 stone. He wore a ridiculously oversized basketball singlet, low slung jeans and was laden with layers of gold jewellery. The most ridiculous thing about him though was his hair, which had been corn-rowed. This get-up with his NHS glasses made him look like an idiot and a half - she was the idiot and he was the half.

Throughout the segment they tried to get the audience to whoop and jeer at certain points, but most of them were OAPs on a day out and were dozing off. The show was dreary to say the least. The only thing that kept me from dozing off myself was a lady sitting behind me who kept coughing throughout the interview. It was niggling away at me and making me more and more irritable. The more I tried to ignore it, the more I was waiting for the next bout, and she was always able to deliver.

After half an hour of ceaseless coughing, I couldn't take anymore, so I politely turned round and asked her if she would like me to go and get her a glass of water. She declined and politely thanked me, saying she would make every effort to stop. Those three minutes were the most peaceful of the whole afternoon. Then she started up again. I was by this point a man on the edge. In a hard-fought battle, I finally turned my concentration to the stage.

Scott was up and out of his chair, dissing Michelle for being a 'lame-ass ho', although it just didn't sound right with a Midlands accent. Then he confessed that he had been 'laying with another brother' to which the host took great pleasure in welcoming to the stage Michelle's brother. At this point the excitement in the studio was at an all-time high and several people managed a polite round of applause. One of the producers stood up to face the audience and had a hand-written card which read "Boo! Hiss!". Several people made half an effort, but it really didn't carry.

Michelle however was giving her all to her performance, throwing her arms about in a rage - though she looked more like a puppet being operated by someone above. Scott was canoodling with Michelle's brother, Kevin (who was as fat as he was thin) and then we broke for a commercial break.

As the show started up again, so did my coughing friend. I tried to alert her to my frustration by turning round sharply and tutting quite loudly, but she didn't get it. I was no longer interested in what was happening on stage, I was trying to think up ways to murder the lady behind me. Ten to fifteen minutes went by and the coughing was becoming worse, so I could do little else but stand up, turn round and scream quite loudly, that if she didn't shut the fuck up, I was going to take my rucksack, empty it of all the contents, bundle it up into a tight ball and then shove it right down her throat. She was shocked, I was shocked but it turns out most of the audience agreed with me and now not only applauded me, but the ones who were able to, gave me a standing ovation. I took my cheers and settled back into my seat before being plucked from it by security and ejected from the studio. I swear I had no idea the show was going out live.

I decided to relocate to the kitchenware aisle, as the security guard looked like he was about to pounce - plus I thought it might be best to shove something else into my basket for appearance sake. As I strolled along, I casually dropped a packet of whatever was nearest to me into my basket, letting it lay there among the other random things I had no intention of actually buying. Luckily this wasn't a big store, so if Mr Incredible was here, he wouldn't be too hard to spot. I took a little walk to the checkout area but did a double-take when I saw the store manager who practically accosted me last week for wrecking his display of chocolate biscuits. As I turned, a little too quickly, I lost my balance, putting my arm out to stop my stumble. The floor was notoriously slippery and my Gucci Chelsea boots were doing little to steady me (but they did look fabulous). As I reached out for support, I knocked a few small jars of vegemite, which began to topple about like drunks on a binge-drinking session. For a moment everything went quiet and the jars seemed to sway in slow motion. I chanced a quick look to the store manager who was looking at me through squinted eyes and I felt hot all of a sudden – an all-too-familiar feeling. Looking back to the jars, the swaying was slowing and it looked like they weren't going to fall after all. My senses were back to normal and everything was calm again. The store manager looked away sharply and I exhaled, grateful that I didn't break something else. Pausing a moment, I contemplated my moment of luck and as I turned around to make my merry way, I walked straight into a shopper causing her to drop what she was carrying; unfortunately for me it was a bottle of red wine. With a loud smash from the bottle, timed perfectly with a loud expletive from me, shards of dark green glass went sliding in every direction, washed along by a syrupy, maroon lake. My right leg was saturated with red wine – and all I could shout out was "Westwood trousers!" to an uncaring audience.

After my second berating this week from a snotty-nosed store manager, I had to pay for the bottle of wine. Great, £13.99 and I didn't even like red fucking wine! I wasn't happy and was half tempted to just discard the basket and leave but I was much too concerned at drawing greater attention my way, so I turned and walked back down to the end of the store, looking for somewhere else to dump it. As I turned back toward the produce aisle, I was suitably stunned when I saw Mr Incredible fingering the courgettes. Excitement got the better of me and I couldn't stop the smile from spreading over my face. I had to calm down; if he looked up now and saw me grinning like a remedial among the lettuces while clutching my basket to my chest, it would surely put him off. Ok, I was calm and made my way to go and get a courgette. I walked over next to Dylan and vacantly reached down into the crate, selecting a courgette. I dropped it in my basket and pretended to be nosing through the mushrooms in the next display. Dylan looked up and stared straight ahead, sniffing. Maybe he had a cold? Oh no shit, it was my leg – I stank of wine. Damn, perhaps I should try to sneak away before he noticed me – then I wouldn't have to go through the embarrassment of explaining why one of my legs was sopping wet and I smelt like Amy Winehouse. Slowly, he turned to face me and to my surprise, a smile spread across his face. He looked great when he smiled – not a wrinkle in sight.

"Hey there, toilet roll man right?"

Laughing to cover my humiliation, "Err, yeah, heh heh, that's me!"

"Wow, you look – great!" he said, with a mixed expression on his face as he checks me over.

I looked down at my attire, "Oh, this old thing?!"

Dylan paused then spoke. "Westwood?"

"Yeah!" this guy is hot AND has good taste in clothes. *Marry me!!*

He paused again. "Cabernet Sauvignon?"

I looked confused, then realised he was talking about my leg. "Oh, um, it might be? Some old alcoholic decided to throw a bottle of wine over me, it wasn't my choice. If it was up to me I'd have gone for a nice Pinot." Dylan laughed again and his eyes seemed to twinkle. The conversation ground to a sudden halt and I was racking my brain to think of something to say when I blurted out one of the worst double entendres I had ever imagined.

"I bet this would put a smile on Delia's face!" I exclaimed, holding up a courgette before me, but meaning it quite innocently.

"Sorry?" he said sounding alarmed.

"Delia. I bet she knows how to use this." Then I realised what I had misconstrued and tried to stammer my way out of it. "I mean, not that she would ever, ever….with a courgette…certainly not…that's what butternut squash are for" I added, trying to turn it into a joke. It didn't work. Thankfully he tried to swing the conversation back to some kind of normality.

"Um, what are you making tonight then?" he said, glancing into my basket. "Oh, I erm…ok." he trailed off, looking up and smiling at me with a momentary look of panic on his face.

What was wrong with him? I glanced down and checked out my own basket, as I hadn't the faintest notion what I'd been throwing in there since I began my stakeout. Bollocks, no wonder he looked scared - even I was put off. What moron goes shopping to buy rubber gloves, olive oil and one insanely large courgette? What must he think?

"You know what?" I said placing my basket on the floor, "I can't even make up something to explain this – I know it looks weird, but I'm just going to be honest."

Dylan rested his basket on the crate of courgettes and gave me his full attention – I wished he wouldn't have, it was a warm day and he was wearing a tight singlet. I could see a fine tuft of mousey blond hair creeping over his neckline and his biceps were all too inviting. How was I supposed to concentrate when I was stood before possibly the most beautiful man I had ever seen?

"I just had to say that since that…fiasco the other day, I mean, it was totally a misunderstanding. You see, I spotted you and I wanted to say hi – I know that's really forward and stuff but I thought what the heck, and so I decided to chase you. Well, not chase – that's quite strong. And weird right, I mean, who wants to be chased around a supermarket by a strange man? Well, actually, if I give it some thought….no, just joking. Erm, where was I? Oh yes, well…"

Dylan didn't reply – he crossed his arms and waited for me to get to the point. Did I even have one?

"So – yeah, it all went a bit tits up and then you said hi, and I wanted to talk more but, well to be honest, I didn't have a clue what to say and let's face it – who wants to be chatted up by a man on his knees in a supermarket with a brown stain on his arse? Well, if I give *that* some thought…oh, I've used that joke already…"

I saw frowning.

Thankfully after a few awkward moments, he stepped in to rescue me from making myself look even more of a fool, which at that point, I didn't think was possible.

"It's ok" he said half laughing. "I was glad you chased me! I actually spotted you too and wanted to say hello."

"You did?"

"Yeah, I saw you but you looked a little busy, trying to hide the cakes and stuff in your trolley" he said, ending with a handsome smile. Sucking in my gut I smile too and shrug it off.

"But – that doesn't matter now does it" he continued, flashing me another of his trademark smiles. "We're chatting and that's the main thing."

I nodded and was about to go for the kill by routinely giving him my number, but before I could say another word we were interrupted.

"Are you going to be all day or can we finally leave?" said an older voice, placing a hand on his shoulder. I recognised him. It was the perverse father-figure who was manhandling my future husband last week. Bugger, surely he must be his boyfriend? I looked away and gave them a moment's privacy, hating every second of it. The old man sauntered off to join the *five items or fewer* queues with his heavy trolley and began to unload. Dylan turned to me and looked forlorn.

"Sorry about that – he's…er…"

"It's ok – no need to explain – I should be getting on with my shopping. I think I'll get some nice cheese to rub on my other leg and make a nice after-dinner snack out of this mess at least."

"No – it's not what you think, we're not – I mean, well, it's hard to explain but…"

"Dylan! Hurry up please; you know I have a colonic at three!" the old man interrupted again. Dylan nodded curtly to the old man in response and turned back to me.

"It's not what it seems" he tried again, looking me dead in the eye. "But I can't go into it now." Biting his lip, he held his breath a second while he thought. "Rubicon in Soho, Friday afternoon, 12 o clock - lunch ok?" he said as he strutted off to help unload the shopping. "Oh, and have fun with your courgette!" he threw over his shoulder and gave me a cheeky wink. As I turned away, I couldn't keep the excitement within me and I gently swiped out with my foot at a small pineapple that has fallen loose from its display. My kick must have been stronger than I imagined because it went hurtling across the kiwis and into a crate of oranges, setting the whole lot cascading down onto the floor. I could see the store manager walking my way, flanked by the security guard – here we go again.

Some seedy bar, Kings Cross. 2:12am.

The afternoon couldn't have been worse; I'd had 2 clients today and was worn out, more emotionally than physically.

My lunch-time client was Stu; 37 and a burly labourer who I scarily found out, still lived with his elderly mother. I turned up at his address, pressed the buzzer and found myself being greeted by a little old lady who was wearing a caftan and smelled strongly of lavender. She literally whisked me in, threw me on the flowery sofa and started talking to me about her love of music. I was shocked to say the least, but polite enough to go along with the conversation which revolved around Max Bygraves and Frank Sinatra. Then she started warbling in an off-key, old lady way. Just before she could launch into *My Way,* Stu bounded down the stairs and thankfully snatched me away from her without a word. I think she carried on singing even though I had left. Thank God, I was starting to think I had the wrong address and was going to be sung to death.

As Stu and I we were getting it on upstairs in the box room (I on my back and my legs pointing in all directions) there was a knock at the bedroom door. From out in the hallway we were politely offered tea or coffee and some lemon drizzle cake. Stu and I looked at each, eyes wide. Just as I yelled out a very panicked 'No thank you!' Stu shouted 'Yep, be down in a minute'. Suddenly the doorknob turned and the door creaked open. I didn't know what to do when in plodded Stu's mother, placing down a tray of goodies on the bedside table next to us. She took one look at Stu who had me hoisted up in the air, one brief look at me laying there with all my wobbly bits wobbling and simply said "Ooh, that takes me back!" broke into something by Cliff Richard and then left the room.

Later on after I had left Stu to have words with his mother, I met my other client who, funnily enough, was also named Stuart. However, this Stuart was a college boy. I had foolishly imagined some kind of sporting college jock or rugby stud or similar, but when I got to his place I was doubly shocked. Firstly, Stuart didn't look the hard man of sport I had envisioned with his bushy ginger hair and face full of acne. He must have been nine stone and as white as a sheet. The second shock was that he didn't live with friends or parents, but in the Halls of Residence. Students everywhere! I was surrounded by computer geeks and science boffins. I took a deep breath, swallowed my pride and followed him to his dorm, which thankfully was a single. The sex was horrible - awkward, sterile and bony. No sooner had it started than it had finished and he erupted like a usually-dormant volcano. Stuart ran to the communal toilets to get some toilet paper to mop up and then paid me in loose change which he scavenged from every pocket and shelf in his room.

In my defence, given today's appalling clients, I was driven to drink. Tonight had really only started out as a quiet couple with my friends, Jacqui and Debs and that was all good and well in theory, but given my history with these two girls, a quiet couple was as unlikely as me visiting a client to share a nice meal.

We met in Knightsbridge early in the evening, and after our sixth or seventh drink together, the conversation had started to get louder and the stories more crude. An audible *tut* from the next booth had moved our focus away from bad sex stories and onto blatant attacks on the stuck-up patrons. The manager then came over and asked us to finish our drinks and leave – always a sign of a good night when we get thrown out of a bar.

As Jacqui was telling us how it would be a good idea to grab the drinks hose and shove it up the manager's arse, she leaned over to take a sip of her vodka and coke, but accidentally poked herself in the eye with the straw. This could have been played down by a simple hand over the eye and rushing to the toilet, but Jacqui wasn't a girl of half measures, so instead, she opted for maximum drama and screamed like a banshee, which of course sent Debs and me into fits of laughter.

Jacqui and I had been through a lot together over the years, she being the only friend from school who I had actually wanted to keep in contact with. I remembered meeting her just after I had turned 15; we were outside the principal's office at school, where I had been sent for detention purpose. Stupidly, I had tried my first and only cigarette, sneaking into the toilets with possibly the hottest guy at school, Jason. He played hockey and had a body to die for and after seeing me with my cigarette thought it a good way to waste his free period. Personally, I was there hoping that one fag would lead to another, but it wasn't to be. The bathroom door suddenly banged open and Jason scampered out the access window at the back of the bathroom, leaving me standing there by myself in a cubicle, holding a still-smouldering cigarette as Mr Johnson came into view. After I was frog-marched to the principles office, I saw Jacqui and mustered up some courage to ask her why she was there. Her detention had been issued for similar reasons, having been caught in the toilets in a slightly similar situation, only that she had been going down on the captain of the school football team; Christopher McGuire, while his girlfriend was in an English class.

67

As we sat there out the front of principal Suffolk's office waiting for our respective lectures, I remembered feeling petrified that the school would call my parents and they'd ship me off to Australia or some other place where dirty criminals are sent.

Conversely, Jacqui and Chris were talking about where and when they were next to meet up. I had thought that Jacqui was the epitome of coolness. Without being too obvious, I studied her as she flirted and chatted with him. Her school dress was tailored three inches above regulation length and was complete with home-made plunging neckline. The shirt underneath her dress was unbuttoned and its sleeves rolled up. To top off the look, her hair was dyed a vicious blue-black.

She noticed me looking at her so I filled her in on my story (obviously it was unexpected to find someone of my prissiness to be outside the principal's office). We shared in further details, stories of our crimes, my mouth hanging agape while she elaborated on hers. I finished mine by telling her that I much rather would have been in her shoes, and then gave a sly wink to the football captain. This totally repulsed him, but Jacqui revelled in the humour of it all, and adopted me immediately. After all, having a gay friend in school was one of the most subversive things she could do to her catholic parents. We'd been inseparable ever since that moment, complementing each other so well in our differences.

While Jacqui was vying for everyone's attention in the bar, pointing out that she nearly ruptured her eye on a straw, Debs, thinking the whole charade was hilarious, laughed so hard she snorted most of her Kir Royale onto her handbag, which in turn made me laugh.

Jacqui was incensed at our lack of compassion and stopped talking to Debs and me - Debs didn't really care because she was more concerned with sponging the cassis from her Dior with a tissue. After the three of us sat there in near silence for fifteen minutes, Jacqui made her excuses and left. Debs and I sat for a further few minutes before Debs rushed after Jacqui, realising she had left her keys at home in her flat and Jacqui had her only spare set.

I hadn't fancied going home, so I had another drink. After chasing these with several Japanese beers, I decided to go for a drunken stumble around the city; I finally decided that any bar would be as good a place as any to continue my solo bender. The copious amounts of alcohol I'd had that evening had well and truly caught up with me as I stood swaying by the entrance. I pushed through the doors to the club, my eyes rolling around in my head, trying to adapt to the dull lighting. Stumbling over to the bar, I ordered a beer, giving my best performance of a sober man "Yes my good fellow, may I have a bereer...beer". Obviously, there had been slow takings at the place tonight as the barman dismissed my obvious drunkenness and placed a bottle down in front of me.

I opened my eyes wide and tried to focus on the blurry figures around me as I sipped from my bottle. A large, tubby man with a tiny goatee and a tight-checked shirt had been looking at me for about ten minutes now and he wouldn't look away. I hadn't held his gaze – honestly, I'd have been too scared to. However, I had quite a dilemma; the guy who was stood next to him was very sexy and I wanted to get off with him, but I couldn't give him the eye as I was likely to be mauled by the wrong one. I'd only been to this club once before, many years ago but I knew there were two floors – and it appeared I was on the duller of the two. I went to sit down, but the stool next to me had a rather interesting white stain that I didn't really wish to sit on - all the other seats were taken.

I didn't know why I was still drinking, I'd drunk so many that I couldn't actually taste anymore, in fact, my throat felt so sore I should've really gone home, but that cute piece of trade who I wanted to get off with was now heading downstairs. I had to follow, but was gripped with fear; I knew what sort of things went on down there and I wondered if I should. Deciding against it and forcing myself to believe he was just some bit of arse anyway; I finished my drink and made a move to head home. As I did, I suddenly saw that the scary guy who had been eyeing me up all the time I'd been there was now waddling over to me – it was definitely time to make my escape. As I neared the exit, I heard my favourite song of all time pumping through the floorboards from below – it would've be criminal for me not to have gone down to appreciate it. I ventured down the creaky wooden staircase, the already-poor light was slowly being snatched away from me and I found myself immersed into near pitch blackness. It took me a while for my eyes to adjust to the darkness, so I stood in the corner, not wanting to make any sudden movements in case I was raped. Ten or so minutes must had passed and when I was sure I could see at least see silhouettes, I prised myself from the wall and tried to take a wander, pathetically trying to identify which dark form was the eye candy from upstairs. The music was deafening, letting me sing as loudly as I could. While I groped around in the dark like a child playing Blind Man's Bluff, I found myself getting more and more infuriated. Then I saw something shocking; it was bound to happen - someone had slipped and was hunched over on the floor, moaning. I wondered what the health and safety insurance was like - I hoped for their sake they were insured up to the glitter balls. I marched over to help this poor individual, but from what I could make out it looked as though someone was already stood behind him, gripping him around the waist.

Oh, how rude!

Moving away quickly, there was a sliver of light coming from what I presumed was a toilet, so I thought it best for me to go and splash my face before leaving. Just before I got there, there was a hand on my crotch and it certainly wasn't mine. I froze momentarily before calmly removing it, then continuing into the bustling toilet area.

The first sink I saw was free and I hoped to fill the basin with water, however, the lack of a plug wasn't helping. I cupped my hands and splashed my face a few times, helping me to relax. As I stood to dry my face, who was there but the stalker from the bar, just grinning at my reflection in the mirror ahead. Without hesitating, his hand reached for his zipper. I needed to do something immediately, and screaming like a big girl simply wasn't an option here. Without turning around, I put on my gigolo hat and spoke to his reflection.

"I'm glad you caught up with me – I've wanted you all night. Now, are you gonna give it to me then?" I asked in my smuttiest voice.

He didn't speak – I wasn't sure that he knew how, but simply nodded while fishing around inside his pants.

"Good – and don't worry about my little friends – I can give you the name of something very effective to get rid of them." I said while I scratched furiously at my genitals. His eyes traced down to my groin and he looked mortified. "You know, it's not easy finding someone brave enough to touch me down there since the infestation, but you look like you're big and ugly enough to take care of yourself. I mean, what are a few bloodsucking parasites to a strapping young lad like you? Come on sex-pig, I want it and I want it *now*!"

I didn't even have to say another word; he was zipping up and fleeing like an oversized pudding in leather trousers. I smiled to myself contentedly for a minute or two before I realised several disgusted looking punters eyeing me in horror as they slid their way out of the room. It was definitely time for me to make my exit and stagger home to bed.

Inside someone's wardrobe, somewhere in West London.

I shouldn't have been enjoying this, but as I listened to the muffled arguing floating around the room on the other side of the door I was crouched at, I found myself thoroughly appreciating the situation.

"Where is the little slut? When I find her I'm going to KILL HER!"

"Darling, there ISN'T anyone here – why don't you LISTEN?"

"Because you're home on a Wednesday afternoon when you should be at a conference in Bristol...AND YOU'RE NAKED!"

Suddenly the argument had softened; it probably moved downstairs while the search for the mystery slut went on.

When I first met with Andrew, he had seemed like the average, horny businessman.

"And you're quite discreet, are you?" was all he kept asking me as he drove us to his four-bedroom townhouse in leafy Richmond. I assured him I was very discreet. It was funny really how it turned out; maybe if he ever decided to call up someone for sex in the future, he would ensure that his wife wasn't going to return home unexpectedly from a hard afternoon's shopping to find him splayed out on the John Lewis divan, wearing nothing but a look of total arousal.

Far be it from me to blow my own trumpet, but I had just been blowing Andrew's and I had to say, given him some of the best oral sex I think he had ever encountered. For me, it was less than enjoyable; it was really just a bit too hairy. Fighting the urge to gag (several times), I made out like I didn't ever want to suck anything else other than his dick, and he pretty much seemed to buy it. To my shock, I discovered that Andrew had a strong desire for something that I hadn't yet come across in my line of work. The chances of that were slim, since I had to come across everything else at least one way or another. Andrew was into nipple play, or tit-torture I recall it being described in some magazine. He wanted me to pinch them hard, probably with a crocodile clip or something. It wouldn't surprise me if he was one of those guys who could attach a family size pack of wooden clothes pegs to them and not even wince. The thought of it made me want to giggle, but I had to play along.

During our act of oral love, he would murmur something or other inaudibly and then reach for one of his pink tax-discs to give them a tug.

Personally, I had a strong dislike of nipples and mine for instance, have never worked; not that I was entirely sure what men's nipples were supposed to do. But if anyone decided to tweak mine in the name of fun and games, he would surely leave with a broken limb. This dislike of nipples stemmed back to one of the first sexual experiences I'd had with a guy who wanted to lick mine. Admittedly it wasn't a bad feeling, almost pleasant in a way, but when they failed to respond to his tongue, he decided to try something else. He learned the hard way that if the tongue wasn't working, then the teeth definitely weren't.

"Pull them!" Andrew had said with desperation in his voice. I stopped mid-suck and had looked up with confusion on my face.

"My nipples - pull them, please!"

"Oh, are you sure?"

"Yes, yesyesyes, pull on my tits!" he pleaded.

I moved myself up to his waist level and sat beside him on the bed. He was lying flat out with his eyes screwed tightly shut. I had daintily put my thumb and forefinger around one of his wormy looking nips and gave a slight tug. Andrew spoke in a fast, breathy voice.

"Harder. Pull on my tits, harder, pull on my tits". It was like a chant for the under-exposed to normality. It had seemed like a fitting time to have a small baying crowd holding banners and megaphones in the room, shouting encouraging nipple-related remarks. I tightened my grip on his nipple and gave a hard yank.

"Pull on my tits!"

"I AM!" I said through gritted teeth, pulling with a lot of strength – Andrew loved it. I had the feeling I was going to pull so hard, the poor thing might snap off in my hand, and I wanted to stop. Thankfully I didn't have to continue this bizarre act for too long. The sound of tyres rolling up the gravel driveway had made Andrew sit bolt upright.

"Shit, it's Yvonne – hide!"

I looked around the master bedroom – the bed we were on was an ensemble; no chance of me slinking underneath it. There was a clothes hamper in the corner, but only the canvas foldaway type – I doubt it would have taken my weight. That only left the wardrobe, obvious choice but it was either I hide in there or I explain to Yvonne why I was straddling her Andrew on a wet Wednesday afternoon. I opened the door and pushed back some hangers and frilly garments that I prayed were Yvonne's. Outside I could hear Andrew stumbling to get dressed, then him cursing as he kicked the corner of the bed in his panic.

Suddenly…"Andrew? Is that you?"

"Shit, shitshitshitshitbugger – shit"

What followed can only be described as several minutes of continuous, high-pitched screaming; who it was coming from cannot be confirmed.

"Swine, bloody swine. Margo *told* me she'd seen you in town with a trollop – yes, that's the word she used Andrew – trollop. Who is she then, hmm? Office tart? You bastard!"

"Darling, let me explain…"

"Don't you *dare* darling me, you pathetic toad. Mother was right, I should have divorced you after I found out you only drove a BMW 3 series, but I stayed because I ……loved you" she sobbed.

"But Yvonne, darling…I…"

"How could you do this to me after all we've been through together?" She snivelled in a bubbly-sounding voice. "We've had more dramas than *anybody* I know; we've more ups and downs than a *bloody* yoyo and now this, *this*! How am I supposed to deal with this, hmm? I've just spend bloody hours in Peter Jones because they forgot to order that fabric to recover the pouffe!" she added, nearly shrieking at the end of her diatribe.

Her posh, shrill voice seemed almost comical; I couldn't see her, but I imagined her wearing a high-collared frilly blouse with pearl buttons, a sensible tweed skirt and some nice court shoes from Dolci's.

The arguing continued downstairs and then I heard the front door open. More shouting came from outside for a few moments more, interrupted by bouts of snotty crying and stamping of sensibly-shoed feet. Finally, a car door opened and slammed shut, before an engine roared to life and the car took off down the driveway.

Slow and heavy footsteps mounted the stairs and into the master bedroom. Andrew opened the wardrobe door and it suddenly struck me how hot it had been I there as the cool air hit me in the face.

"I think we should...finish this for today. Maybe in the future...erm..."

Darn. I was just starting to enjoy that. I loved a bit of good old fashioned arguing. I gathered up my clothes that had been shoved into the hamper in a moment's panic, and we both dressed in silence. Taking my pay, I descended the stairs and left.

Dr Finlay's Front Door - Olympia.

I had been stood on Dr Finlay's front step for approximately ten minutes trying to think of something witty to greet him with. I hadn't been so nervous for a long time - well, except for that time when I was 'Puss in Boots' in the school pantomime. I was hardly a child actor – you know, those cute little tykes on American soap operas, the little precocious bastards you want to strangle. No, acting was definitely not in my blood. However, because I was such a cute child they decided to throw me into the lead role. I didn't ask for it.

I remembered sitting at the dinner table with my mother, who would quiz me every night on my lines. Why would someone choose to put a child through so many traumas before the age of ten? Looking back, Puss in Boots really wasn't a positive play for children to study; it was based on deception, greed and murder. I supposed it was just a bit like watching Emmerdale but with the added bonus of being able to shout "behind you" on the odd occasion.

Opening night was a freezing December night; all of the extended family had congregated at the school to see me. My Uncle Jim would keep going on about how I was to be the budding star of the family and how one day he could sit back and retire on the many millions of pounds I'd be earning, then he'd laugh. Sure it was funny – funny for an old fucker who made nothing of his life; there was nothing funny to a nine year old who thought that he had to succeed enough to support fifteen relatives. Even to this day, I could still remember the heavy, musty smell of the dirty, red velvet stage curtain and hearing the murmuring crowd beyond. I was the only one on stage as the child playing the Marquis of Carabas was off sick; my teacher didn't think to get another child to learn the lines. So I just stood there, waiting for the start of the play but all I could think of was how ridiculous my cat costume looked. With a budget of a about a fiver and a mother who couldn't sew, I really didn't have a chance. The stage props were basic to say the least. Centre stage was the mill - a large cardboard box with a bicycle wheel stuck to it - and to the right, a palm tree from last year's production of Arabian Nights.

Mrs. Laney started to play the piano as the curtain was hoisted up, leaving an identical thin curtain of dust in its place. The musical score was no John Williams effort either, considering she was half-blind and she was missing an F sharp on her piano. To ensure she wouldn't have to use that note, she transposed the entire score into a minor key, thus making it sound more like the score from *Schindler's List*.

There was no reassuring applause or encouraging smiles, just begrudged parents and older siblings staring at me. I was terrified and the overhead lights were making me sweat. I didn't even know what my first line was, I remembered the headmistress in the wings on my right whispering harshly for me to start when someone in the crowd yelled out "Get on with it, you big pussy poofta!" I stood there, blinked twice and then wet myself.

You'd think the most embarrassing part of the fiasco would have been the next day at school when the other kids had gotten their hands on the leftover production posters, crudely changing them from 'Puss in Boots' to 'Piss in Boots', then stuck them all over my desk – children really were mean little fuckers. No, the worst part of all was me having to sit in the emergency room for three hours after the play, waiting for a nurse to remove my whiskers which my mother had super glued to my face. Apparently she was worried they would fall off half way through the show and decided to take preventative measures.

"Hi Rich...I noticed you standing out here – are you okay?" Dr Finlay said looking down at me as he held the door open.

"Hi there" I said lamely, looking up and noticing that my arm was still raised and my finger was still hovering centimetres from the bell. I wondered how long I had been stuck in that pose for; the fact that I had pins and needles suggested a while.

Dr Finlay gave me a quick peck on the cheek before ushering me in to the hallway and closing the door behind me. I followed him down the communal hall and into his ground-floor apartment, watching his buttocks jiggle up and down as he strode.

"So...er...Nigel" I ventured "how was work today?" I still couldn't get past his name. It was very embarrassing when he called a couple of days back, and I had responded to his greeting with a curt "Nigel...Nigel who? Sorry, I think you have the wrong number". It was only when he reminded me of the blatant hard-on in his office that I twigged who it was. After referring to him three times as Dr Finlay, he asked me why I was being so formal. I spouted some lame story about the fact my old milkman was named Nigel and he used to scare me. Then I had asked him if he were called Nige as a nickname. However, having realised in my head that I didn't even like that, I went as far as to say "Can I call you N for short?"

"Yeah my day was good - had to lead a gastroscopy demonstration in the hospital today – lots of interns there. How's your job...uh..." he trailed off lamely, looking around to change the subject.

"Oh yeah, great actually – mucho shagging and blew a few guys yesterday. One had the most incredible need for an electric hedge-trimmer" I said laughing, hoping to break the ice. It didn't.

He then proceeded to make some more pointless chit-chat as he led me in to the most beautiful living room I'd seen outside of a magazine. It was painted a rich dark olive, offsetting the gorgeous maple furniture, making the whole room look as if it was a set from a Sherlock Holmes movie. Apt really, considering Sherlock was one of the all-time iconic bachelors. Personally, I thought he was banging Dr. Watson behind the study door after snorting a few lines and drinking himself into a stupor; a typical Friday evening in gay society.

I walked over to where he was stood in front of a latte-coloured suede sofa; large plush cushions placed strategically on it making it look ever so comfy and inviting. He grabbed a bottle of red that was breathing on the coffee table in front of the sofa and poured two glasses, handing one to me.

"Cheers" I said, perhaps with too much enthusiasm, chinking the glass rather heavily and sloshing some of the wine onto the floorboards, thankfully missing the sofa. "Oopsie daisy" I said, feeling very much like a newcomer to high society.

"Never mind" he smiled, sitting down on the sofa and patting the spot next to him for me. I returned his smile even though I found it one of the most ridiculous things for a person to gesture. Yes, thank you, I can see that you've sat down and I can join you and no, I'm not a dog. However, I didn't say anything as I could easily see myself marrying this man - after arranging him a quick name change by Deed Poll mind you. Begrudgingly, I joined him on the sofa and realising my penchant for clumsiness, decided to hold my wine glass with two firm hands like a toddler, determined not to drink any more as long as I was sitting.

He was staring straight ahead as I chatted to him about the furniture. Truth be told, I didn't know anything about it and I'd noticed that he wasn't really paying attention anyway. "Oh, yes well Ikea does have some lovely flat-pack furniture. Just last week I assembled my own Eighteenth Century style harpsichord with nothing more than a Cuban-heeled shoe to knock in the nails". Before I had a chance to elaborate, he took a daring a chug of his wine and turned to me, his eyes ablaze with lust. Uh-oh, I only had approximately two seconds to put the wine on the table in front of me and, yep, we had lift off.

The typical commencement of a nervous guy in that situation was to either wait for me to start the move or pounce like a frightened animal, fending for his own life. It was actually kind of endearing in a way, knowing that he was nervous as hell and wanted desperately to perform and show me he was capable at this whole thing.

He began kissing me madly, his tongue thrusting into my mouth, his hands fumbling at his shirt buttons. My mouth tightened as I forced back a smile, my hands calmly undoing his shirt buttons from the bottom, working up to meet his hands that were still grappling with the top one. He sat back, pulling at his shirt, trying to get his arms out but managing only to entangle himself further; he looked like a madman trying to escape a straight-jacket. While he was wrestling with himself I unbuttoned my top, not taking my eyes off of him. I ripped it off in true stripper style before he eventually disentangled himself from his own linen prison. Now he was looking at me hungrily, scanning my naked torso as I did the same to him. He sure did keep in shape; there was a lovely leanness to him – muscled without looking like he was trying; like a swimmer. He leant down and clamped onto my mouth again, desperately searching for my tonsils with his tongue. I decided to guide things along before he tried to pull my pants off, doing me an irreparable damage in his haste. I unbuttoned his jeans and guided my hand in. Where was the little bugger? This wasn't boding well for the home team. Getting the message, he got up and pulled down both his jeans and boxers in the one swift motion. I generally liked a guy to stay in his underwear for a while – I enjoyed the anticipation. Looking right into his crotch, I suddenly realised the error of my earlier comment regarding the hedge-trimmer. Damn, he was one of them and looked proportionately shorter with the dense undergrowth that was sprouting up around his dick. I realised he was looking at me expectantly. It was time for me to do what I did best; lie.

"MMMMmmmmm, that's hot N". Ok, N works neither as a name, nor as a hot passionate cry during orgasm, and that was actually the last time I called him by any form of his bloody name.

Laying me down on the couch, he straddled my chest, his hairy bits just dangling over my face. All I could think about was that episode of The Goodies when they were stuck on a submarine and all they had for music was 'A Walk in the Black Forest'.

"You know what" I moaned to Debs as we were standing in line to order our coffees, "It didn't get any bloody better from there". I played with a packet of biscotti I had picked up, and then bit into the wrapping to open it. "I mean really -" I complained, taking a bite of my biscuit, spraying crumbs all over myself. "- he's a doctor! Surely he knows about hygiene and man-scaping. I found myself gagging from the heinous overgrowth and hideous motions he was making. I don't think he'd had sex before, ever, with anyone. I had to call it a night and pretend I wasn't feeling too good." Truth be told, I wasn't feeling good. After going down on someone who hadn't had a shower all day, it made my stomach turn.

Debs knew me better than any of my other friends, and she always listened when I got into one of my moaning sessions about clients/boyfriends/clothes/jobs/anything. We met many moons ago at an office Christmas party. While I was still getting into the swing of being a gigolo and setting up a client base, I decided it would be a good idea to do some office temp work for a little while, whilst I established myself. I bagged a job working as an administrator at a Euston based office and fast made friends with the social groups, after all, there was nothing better than having a group of people who wanted me to offload in a different way. Debs worked in the finance section of an adjacent building, so I never really had a chance to get to know her – but all that changed Christmas 2003.

In early December, we were told that our Christmas party was going to be held in the main lobby of our building. That should have been warning enough to avoid the event. Sure they were getting in a DJ and catering the whole soiree with canapés and drinks, but I couldn't get past the fact that we were all set up next to the guard's station, near the plastic potted plants. I had arrived at the party an hour after it had started, over-dressed and under-impressed. I figured the later I arrived, the less time I had to stay. Thankfully there were a few people there already who I knew and more importantly, liked enough to converse with. It was a typically prescriptive event – drinks, dinner, dancing. I realised just how over-dressed for the event I was in my light grey Italian suit and two hundred pound Italian shoes; most people were wearing the same tired outfits that they wore to work, but with a pair of jazzy earrings or a top button open on their shirt. A few people tried to branch out and doll themselves up for the evening. Some of the more experimental women over forty had attempted to apply makeup but like most people who hadn't cared for themselves in years, they looked hideous. Gillian from human resources looked more like a marionette doll than a human with her rosy red cheeks, light-coloured foundation and spidery eyelashes. Just as the DJ was getting into his full set, I spied the cool crowd in the corner near the bar; Marty, Gordo, Glenn and Lisa. After stocking up on a couple of double G&T's, I made a beeline for them and was immediately introduced to Debs who was chatting with them. During the conversation, I noticed that the dinner tables around the foyer were labelled with pre-set nametags. Without caring who was looking, I rearranged some of them so that the six of us were sitting together - there was no way I was suffering the evening with freaks sitting next to me, boring me about their domesticated lives. Who really cared that their child has just gotten their lilac belt in non-violent self-defence?

The night became more and more of a blur as we drank and laughed. Debs' sense of humour was so in tune with mine – slightly catty, but very clever and dry. One poor guy came up to ask her to dance and she let him have it. Not because he asked her, rather that it was not flattering to be asked to dance by someone when there was a gigantic erection tenting his trousers (though we all agreed afterwards that had he been half cute, it would have been acceptable – if not desirable).

The next thing I remembered I was kneeling on the floor in front of the toilet with the lid closed and snorting coke through a rolled up tenner. I didn't even know whose coke it was, or why I actually wanted to take some. Next moment of lucidity was 3pm the following day as I lay on Debs' bed, still in my previous night's attire. I discovered Debs in her bath tub with the shower curtain ripped off the rail as her blanket. We'd been inseparable ever since.

Of course, as soon as I had met up with Debs at Starbucks, I told her all about the supermarket guy and how we had planned to meet up. She was genuinely pleased for me but told me not to get over-excited. I replied that I knew it was going to be perfect, to which she bit her bottom lip and spoke very calmly and sensibly, telling me that all men were insane and if it did work out, it was inevitable that sooner or later he would break my heart. She wasn't being nasty, just upfront. I had to admit, I kind of saw where she was coming from. Being the insatiable romantic I was it was always good (and protective) to have a friend who was realistic enough to pull me back in line.

I flashed a smile at her as we progressed in the queue for our coffee. "What's with the grin?" she quizzed, giving me a cheeky smile in return.

"Nothing…just that I appreciated you meeting me in my hour of need" I exclaimed.

"Only you, Rich, could call blowing a guy with a small dick and overgrown bush an hour of need. We both laughed and a man behind us shifted uncomfortably. As I continued relaying the story of my night's disaster, I subconsciously scanned the line, looking for anyone of interest.

"Well at least most gay guys take care of themselves" she offered. "Look at straight guys – they are usually the most hairy, hideous and smelly bunch of pricks you'll ever come across…no offence" she added to the guy in front who was looking back over his shoulder at us. Debs was as hopeless as I was in love and she understood the fact that there really was no one out there. Her theory was that all the good people were taken, and the only ones left were the balding, fat guys and the ones who lived with their parents. The guy in front of us stepped up to the counter and ordered his drink. "Grande sugar-free, no-foam, non-fat, decaf soy cappuccino to go."

Debs and I turned to each other; the look we exchanged said it all. If this was all that was left for us to date then I'd rather blow someone off and thank them on the way out the door with a fistful of their cash.

Friday, late afternoon in my flat with a bottle (or two) of wine.

I wasn't usually in the habit of drinking at home and I certainly wasn't in the habit of drinking at home enough to get drunk. Thankfully I'd been drinking some cheap wine, only about 11%. With that being said, I had to stay on the floor a little while longer, just until the dizziness passed.

It was official, today had been a disaster and it started off so well. I was up like the proverbial bird; eager, enthusiastic and willing to get my worm. Today was lunch day with Dylan. I woke at six to realise that was still practically night time, so I crashed for a further hour, though I barely slept and upon seeing the clock strike seven, I leapt out of bed and went straight to the shower, bypassing both my mobile phone and the computer; today was not a day for other men or paying freaks – today was a day for Dylan. I lathered myself in some expensive body wash and whistled a happy tune as if I were some perky housewife from the fifties. I followed the shower with a good breakfast; lots of blended fruits and a big dollop of natural yoghurt - healthy inside equals healthy outside. Next I picked out several outfits, lay them on the bed and chose some getting-ready music, spending far too long contemplating my look for the afternoon. By the end of CD 1 of my two-disc set, I had whittled the choices down to two of my favourite looks; charcoal grey pinstripe Armani trousers, black fitted shirt and tan Chelsea boots; or my all-time favourite pair of bulge-exaggerating Guess jeans, white shirt and fitted grey V-neck Paul Smith sweater. The jeans had done so well when I was getting checked over (literally) by Dr Finlay, so I opted for outfit two.

It was around eleven as I was lacing my trainers. I grabbed my jacket, wallet and keys and headed out the door. It was a fresh morning, the sun was breaking through a little scattered cloud and the sky was bursting with blue – everything felt good.

The bus ride into town was only short so I would definitely make good time. I felt particularly good about myself; all my spots had cleared up, my hair had actually co-operated with my hair gel, and I looked quite dishy, even if I did say so myself. Dylan was a lucky boy.

Upon arriving at Rubicon, I took a seat inside a dimly lit booth, which I deliberately picked because it looked perfect for a smooch and a cuddle. The menu looked great also, but I wasn't very hungry. Looking around I could see all the other first daters enjoying themselves – I got a nice, warm feeling in my tummy. I checked my watch - 11:57am. Nearly time. I signalled for a waiter and ordered myself a Cosmopolitan. Dylan was probably running a little late. I took a deep breath and made myself relax.

I was on my second Cosmo by 12:15pm and getting a little agitated sat there alone looking like a loner. I knew there was only one Rubicon in Soho so he couldn't have gone to the wrong one. I was getting myself a little worked up and had to reassure myself there was a perfectly reasonable explanation, probably tube delays. At that very moment the door swung open quite forcefully, allowing a tall Dylan-sized man to walk in and look around. I couldn't make out if it was him or not so I stood up in case it was. It wasn't, and he joined his lunch date. Looking more than awkward, I sat back down and slugged the dregs of my second Cosmo and before I could raise my hand to order another one, the waiter gestured to me that he already knew what I wanted - cheeky sod.

By 12:58pm, I had drank 4 Cosmos, half a glass of *L'Acqua Frizzante* and eaten a small plate of overpriced bruschetta. Dylan wasn't going to show; it didn't take a scientist to work that out. The waiter, who had been hanging around me since I sat down, waiting for me to order something substantial and expensive, swaggered over to me with a bored look on his face and insultingly asked, "Does sir require a *fifth* Cosmopolitan to compliment his starter?" Had I been more sophisticated and professional – and less drunk, I would have ignored his bitchy remark, paid for my bill and left while I still had an air of dignity left. As it was, I slurred to him that if I wanted to get pissed on my own at lunchtime then it was of no concern to him, and that if he thought he was going to get a tip from me today it would only be for him to get another job as his waiting skills stunk.

I stood up, slapped my money on the table and left the restaurant. As I walked to the bus stop, it hit me that I had been stood up by my Mr Perfect. A tear formed in the corner of my eye and I wiped it away with an angry, speedy hand. The sun was bright that afternoon so I put my shades on and carried on walking. As I headed into the cool air, I tried desperately not to let myself cry, but it turned out that I could do very little but let the tears stream down my cheeks.

Seat 17A, Iceland Air, Flight 451.

To say I didn't fly very well would have been like saying that Eddie the Eagle didn't ski very well. I was petrified to the point that I couldn't get on the plane without a carry-on of duty-free liquor and a carry-on of pharmaceutical dependencies.

Seat 17B, my newest client Gary, was looking at me with abject concern on his face. I was trying my best to be cool, but everything was freaking me out. Two minutes earlier, the lady in 18C dropped her bag with a loud thud, causing me to shriek like a banshee "Everyone off the plane – or at least brace damn you!"

"No really – I'm fine..." I said, chugging back my third straight vodka. The trolley Nazi had refused to serve anything to me, so I had opened my own litre of Absolut to calm my nerves. I thought it was ridiculous that they didn't serve drinks before takeoff. During the flight I could quite appreciate, but why not before? As I sat with the bottle between my legs and my complimentary plastic cup banging about on the armrest, I decided whether I should keep drinking or try to calm down.

Gary had asked me to accompany him on a work retreat to Reykjavik. He worked for Apple and was being sent away on a lush business junket, all expenses paid. In his eyes and mine, it was the perfect excuse for a bit of long distance loving. I'd never been to Iceland before and I had dressed accordingly, but I had to confess I was starting to sweat under my two sweaters, thick-corded trousers and shin-high hiking boots. Why didn't his work send him to Spain, or Greece? Iceland wasn't labelled for its balmy weather, more its barmy people.

As I stared out the window, I saw all the people bustling around outside, making sure the baggage was loaded, the doors were closed and the wings were firmly attached. I looked at my watch and let out a sigh – I supposed three hours for a flight didn't seem like a long time at all, not when I was hurtling through the lower atmosphere in a pressurized tin can. It was time for another drink. I poured another generous airline cupful and offered Gary one, which he politely refused. I put his tray down for him and put my drink on it while I rummaged through my trusty maroon, zip-up bag of pills. I unzipped it and looked at all the tablets it held for something to help my situation. I'm no hypochondriac, but there were pills for every medical situation; diarrhoea, headaches, hay fever, colds, insomnia. Oh and I also had pills for menstrual cramps (for when I travelled with Debs and Jacqui). They always made fun of me for being so over-packed and cautious, but when we all got Delhi-Belly in Morocco once; they were begging me for my stash of Imodium. Unfortunately, I hadn't packed anything for travel sickness – must remember those for next time. Picking up a jar of muscle relaxants, I decided they would surely do something to help; after all, the word relax was part of their description. It advised for one pill every four hours. Well, the flight was only just over three, and taking into consideration the altitude level as well as the effects of air pressure on the human body, I took three, and one for luck.

The ceiling was quite intriguing. Lots of large coloured squares that had been joined together by plastic strips, which were running horizontally and vertically along the ceiling - it looked like a giant artistic chess board. Startled out of my hazy daydream I sat up and looked around inquisitively to see a myriad of backpacks. Where the fuck was I and why was I laying on a bunk bed? I pulled out my phone to see what time it was, but had trouble focusing on it, unable to make out the numbers – probably the vodka I thought. I must've been getting too old for this. As I squinted harder I saw just how late it was. Jesus, Mary and Joseph – I left Heathrow eleven hours ago. I looked up and around the room, thankful that no one else was present, not even Gary. Given I was lying alone in a hostel room didn't instil much confidence.

I had to sort myself out. First thing I needed was a shower. Actually I needed more sleep and a bacon sandwich, but since that wasn't practical, a shower it was. I stank of plane, vodka and God-only-knew what else. I looked around the room in a slight panic before calming down when I saw my luggage at the end of the bunk. Even in my inebriated state I had managed to keep everything with me. This could have been a whole lot worse. Yes, worse than waking up alone in a hostel, not being able to see clearly. I slid off the bunk and felt myself ache all over – God, must have been some party. I grabbed the towel that was hanging over the metal bed-end and sniffed it to make sure it was clean. Thankfully I had some flip-flops in my bag, thinking I would have needed them for the hot-springs and day-spas that Gary and I were planning to visit. I had presumed the days of showering in a communal bathroom were long in the past. After picking up a handful of clothes and my toiletries bag, I left the room in search of the bathroom. As I was walking down the corridor, two girls walked past me, staring as they went. I could hear their furious whispering as they passed, probably because I was too old and I should be in some five-star hotel by this time in my life. Surely I should've been earning enough to move up in the world, at least to a B&B.

The bathroom didn't have a door; it was just an obvious separate room from the hallway as it was painted a hideous pea green colour that looked more like phlegm green. Poking my head inside, I looked around, worried that I was going to have to haggle with some tourist for use the solitary shower. Thankfully, there were at least a dozen lined up along the left of the room, just before the toilet cubicles. The sinks were to my right, underneath a room length mirror, which I naturally glanced into as I ventured further in. I stopped in horror at the thing that was glaring back at me. With a half-audible shriek I dropped everything I was holding onto the lino and ran to examine more closely in the mirror. My face was bruised beyond belief, my eye was black and dark green and I had a purple swollen bottom lip that was numb to the touch - in fact, my whole face seemed to be numb. Oh God, oh God, oh God...my face, my beautiful face.

Horrified that I was now pulling off a near-perfect resemblance to the Elephant Man I bustled all my stuff into the shower cubicle at the end of the bathroom and pulled the curtain across. I sat on a stool near the shower recess and stared at the tiles on the ground. *How the hell did I*...and before I finished the thought I knew the answer. Like a speeding train, memories came rushing back into my head, each one even more gruesome than the last. A whole stream of very bad memories came flooding into my consciousness, my eyes growing wider as I remembered the myriad of stupid things I had achieved in the past half day. I closed my eyes tightly, running through the thoughts, putting them back into some sort of order and tried to remember what happened.

After I had taken the muscle relaxants on the plane, the rest of the flight was the most blurry of my memories. However, some parts of it stood out for me. I remembered finishing the bottle of vodka quite quickly, then wandering the plane looking for a cigarette from someone. I don't smoke, but had a craving for tobacco. I also had a craving for duty-free so when the little cart came trundling by I made Gary buy me a carton of Marlborough Lights and two bottles of J-Lo's new fragrance. Oh, and I also remember having sex with one of the flight attendants in the tiny bathroom: that would explain some of the bruising around my knees and thighs.

I also remembered Gary cracking the shits with me and leaving the plane without me. The whole customs/airport experience was a blur. The next thing I remembered was sitting in the back seat of a cab, slurring to the cabbie that I wanted a cheap place to stay in Recky Vik and brandishing my JLo fragrance like it was some kind of weird plane trophy. It turned out that nowhere was cheap to stay; just increasing levels of expense. As I had expected Gary to pay for most things, I hadn't brought a great deal of money with me just about twenty quid sterling and my MasterCard.

I remembered checking into a hostel and dumping my stuff before another quick drink, then heading out into town to see what was going on. Being the socialite I was, I had mingled through the streets, striking up conversation with people by shouting very loudly to no one in particular the words *Hurdy Gurdy Gurdy*. My bumbling Icelandic could have gotten me into a lot of trouble, but thankfully, for the most part the Nordic people seem to be kind and gentle. Or maybe they decided it was less painful to let me drink myself to death. Then, in some bar, I remembered hitting it off with a couple of lesbians, both with crazy, curly hair and who were coincidently from London. They were on their way to a gay wedding in the middle of town. Well, I love a good party and next thing I remembered I was sitting between a lesbian and a young guy dressed in leather pants and braces. I was witnessing the marriage of Stefan and Randy, and giggling to myself (and out loud) throughout. Randy was a New York Jew who was emaciated and had a big smile and his partner, Stefan, was a burly Viking with quite a beard. The ceremony vows from what I could remember, took place under one of those Jewish-style canopies, but in my pissed up state kept referring to as the 'tent for midgets'. As the vows came to an end I remembered standing up and applauding which wasn't very suitable as the happy couple had decided upon a ceremony for each culture to celebrate. I plonked myself back into my chair realising the second Icelandic ceremony had just started. Landing with a thump, and just as the couple at the front are declaring their willingness to hitch, I shouted out an untimely "Oopsie!" rather too loudly.

After we all shouted Mazel Tov, there was champagne and I got introduced to the groom and groom. They seemed lovely enough and I presumed both thought I was a long-lost cousin of the other as neither of them questioned my presence. Fast forward a few hours and I was dancing on a table at the reception as an Icelandic Elvis impersonator was rocking and rolling on stage behind me. It got blurrier from there, with a few horrid montages forcing their way into my consciousness: blowjob in the toilet; vomiting over the balcony; screaming match with one of the mother-in-laws for spilling beer all over her; dance-off competition between myself and three teenage Icelandic girls who thought they could out-Vogue me; mad dash for the wedding cake waving a ladle about madly; and a fist fight with Viking groom's brother, shortly followed by a fall down the stairs outside. Apparently there must have been a taxi ride back to my hostel there somewhere, so all in all, not my finest day.

I stood up and turned on the shower, the smell of sulphur overcoming me. Stripping off the rest of my clothes, I balanced them on the stool, careful that none of them were touching the ground. I stepped under the shower, my bruised and battered face and body stinging from the water. I inspected myself and found more bruising on my chest, legs and backside. As there was no soap or shampoo, I just let the water flow over my tired and sore body, wallowing in my own self pity. That was probably one of the lowest points of my life. I didn't have anyone around me, no one to love and a job that really wasn't appearing to be as exciting as I first imagined. Grabbing the wall I leant forward, the water massaging my sore back. As I lowered my head, I start to cry.

Six hours later I was on a red-eye flight back to London courtesy of my MasterCard. At least I was sober and feeling a little more comfortable about flying in a pressurised metal tube. Unlike Juan who revelled in each jaunt overseas, perhaps I wasn't quite ready for client outings beyond Zone 4.

Monday morning at home, still half asleep.

I waddled to the front door and bent down to scoop up the mail, pausing on the way up to fasten my robe which had come loose. As I turned back, half-reading and half-walking, I caught my reflection in the hall mirror; I looked like I had just risen from the dead. My hair was completely flat on one side looking like it has been slicked down and in total contrast, the other side was standing completely on end as if I'd just had a course of electric shock therapy. A tiny hiccup made its way out of my mouth and the taste of lime and salt came flooding into it. I mooched into the kitchen where I dumped the mail on the bench and proceeded to pour myself a tall glass of water from the fridge.

Last night Jacqui and Debs came over for something to eat, slyly bringing an 'old friend' with them. I had known these two deviants long and well enough to know that 'old friend' usually translated into 'single gay man'. No matter how many times I stood up for myself and questioned both their singleness, they attacked me with a barrage of words and abundant quotes about a woman's right to be independent – amazingly turning it around so it was me defending my right to be lonely. Over the years I had learned that it was best not to argue with them and just accept it.

Their tagalong, Simon, was average looking to say the least. His scraggly hair hung lifelessly on his head, falling into small, greasy curls just around his shoulders. Dressed in a red, long-sleeved shirt that did nothing for his pinkish face, jeans which were too baggy and a pair of dirty trainers, he stood in my doorway like an extra on some second rate TV show, hunched over slightly and looking very fearful indeed. I knew from this moment we would not be walking down the aisle together. Jacqui and Debs were fussing around us both, ushering us to both come in, sit on the sofa, and drink my booze as if it were their house and Simon and I were the guests. Eventually, the polite British conversation fell to a stop - Jacqui nudged Debs and gave her a nod of her head, teamed with a look which said "Go on, say something!"

"Simon" started Debs in a trill voice. "How's your job going? Rich, Simon works at MTV, don't you Simon."

He didn't reply – he thought looking at me and smiling an ugly, sheepish smile would win me over. He had thought wrong.

"And isn't it right..." Debs continued, "...that only last week you stood behind Dave Berry and that chap from The Kaiser Chiefs, the one with the big nose?"

Simon again tried his sultry look without saying a word. Did he really need to be sat here? The girls were doing such a good job of telling me about his life, I had yet to hear a single word uttered from his mouth. He was a big, dull reality that I had to endure for God-only-knew how long.

"I've spoken to Dave Berry, he's really nice actually" he eventually piped up, causing me to half choke on my Gin-laced Lambrusco.

"So, what is it you do then at MTV, presenting?" I offered, thinking he might be worth hanging out with on the promise of a night in M*vida.

"Er, well, I work kind of behind the scenes really" he said as he looked at Jacqui and Debs for guidance. They didn't offer any. "It's a small team, but working there is lots of fun and very prestigious – makes the job worthwhile, you know" he trailed off, running his finger around the rim of his glass.

"...Ye-es, so? What is it you do – at MTV? You still haven't told me."

"I er, I work in the industrial...er, well the hygiene...I'm a cleaner."

Simon didn't look up from his glass. I looked to Debs, Debs looked to Jacqui and Jacqui jumped out of her chair, offering refills all round. As the last of the Gordon's splashed into my glass, I had to speak to cut the silence.

"Well, a job's a job" I said defiantly. Simon seemed to stir a little and made eye contact again, still with his sheepish, ugly smile.

"So what did Dave Berry say to you then?" I added.

"He asked me to move because I was standing too close to him. But he was really nice about it. Said my bucket was a bit smelly and that he was about to go an interview Lindsay Lohan, and would prefer it he didn't smell like a dead trout. Nice bloke."

"Yeah, diamond!" I chimed.

From that moment on it was polite chit-chat fuelled by Lambrusco, eight cans of Carling Light and two and a half packets of Rich Tea biscuits. The stir fry had gone to pot.

Simon was actually quite nice to chat to after a fashion. He told us about his cleaning job and which famous people he had seen snorting what in the dressing rooms. Simon's best story was about a famous rapper who was rude to him for being in his dressing room and had thrown an empty glass bottle at him, which narrowly missed. While he was answering a call of nature, Simon paid him back by mixing some Ajax powder into his coke. I was starting to like him.

Debs then suddenly squealed with delight as she remembered she had brought a present with her, and reached into her bag to pull out a bottle of Tequila like a magician pulling a rabbit from a hat. It wasn't unusual for her to carry booze in her bag, in fact, she nearly always had a little bottle of something; 'to pick me up' were her choice words.

I hazily recalled the story when Jacqui's sister was having her daughter baptised and Jacqui and Debs were watching from the front row. Debs had been sipping at an Evian bottle throughout which was actually filled with vodka & lemonade. This only came to light as the ceremony ended and Debs stood up on wobbly legs, offered the vicar ten pounds if she could have a dip in the font as her heating was on the blink and hadn't had a bath in days, before collapsing in a heap of giggles on the floor.

The blurry evening turned into a heavily drunken night and most of the Tequila was gone by 2am. I'd like to say I knew exactly what happened, but I'd be a liar if I didn't say I was horrified and shocked to wake up in my bed with Simon half cradling me; still with that fucking sheepish, ugly smile - even while he slept. More to the point, after this realisation I was even more shocked when I peered down and saw Debs and Jacqui at the other end of the bed, topping and tailing us.

As I sat at the breakfast bar, I finished my glass of water and thumbed through the post. Bill, bill, reminder – ooh, postcard! I knew who it was from without reading it. Most postcards flew through the letterbox brandishing scenes of idyllic summer hot-spots, awash with white, sandy-fringed beaches and peppered with swaying palm trees. When a postcard landed on the mat with a 6ft tanned hunk wearing nothing but a coconut shell and a smile – it could only mean one thing; Juan was somewhere fabulous. It seemed Mauritius was that week's location of choice. From the card I learned that he wasn't with a client, working – he had simply 'taken time out darling, it's just all so stressful' he had scribbled. I lost myself in thought about booking a last minute holiday when the realisation of Reykjavik came flooding back to me. It would be almost unheard of for someone to take two holidays in under a month unless they were a football hero or an ageing rocker, or indeed Juan. I snapped out of my daydream to find Simon standing in the kitchen doorway, patting his tummy. I pointed him to the fridge and let him sort himself out – I was in no mood to play mother.

Everyone eventually left around midday – just before I got a call from Tony Tonsils. I'd like to say he acquired such a moniker from his ability to kiss like a love God, but I couldn't. Tony had the worst case of halitosis imaginable. He paid well though and I always met him armed with a packet of mints. I mused over an excuse or two as Tony and I spoke, but my eyes fell upon my assortment of bills and I decided I wasn't fortunate enough to be able to pick and choose at this current point in time. I looked longingly at the postcard once more before tacking it to the fridge where it became lost among all the others. Then I went to get dressed and prepared myself for Tony.

Like a few of my more interesting clients, Tony had a fetish. His thing was feet – cheesy feet, dirty socks and sweaty trainers to be precise. When we first met and he told me of his proclivity, I was quite shocked and argued my case against it from athlete's foot to running pustules; this only made him want it more. Reluctantly I surrendered and let him take over. It wasn't as bad as I originally thought it would be. All I had to do was lay on the bed while he rubbed, sniffed and sucked my toes. The best way to deal with it was to I pretend I was having a pedicure from a very enthusiastic beautician.

Forty minutes later I rang Tony's buzzer and his nasally voice poured from the intercom. As I made my way up the flight of stairs, I thought to myself that I could actually do with a nice relaxing foot rub, though when I made my pleasantries with him in his apartment, he quite obviously had other plans. Before I was able to whip off my Converse and wiggle my toes, he stood before me with a beautifully wrapped gift. I grabbed it with relish and tore at the shiny paper. Inside was a pair of brand new Nike Air trainers. He said he wanted me to put them on, and then go for a run to get my feet all hot and sweaty. Then he told me how he wanted to sniff the shoes and lick my feet. This turned my stomach for two reasons: one – he was standing far too close and his breath honked something chronic; and two – the thought of doing several laps around the park brought me out in a cold sweat. I tried to blag my way out of it by constantly rubbing at my calf with a pained expression on my face, but every time I tried to avoid it, the thought of my bills came rushing back to hit me in the face. Reluctantly, I stepped into my new bumpers while Tony sat down by my feet to tie the laces.

When I said that I would go along with it as long as he came to the park too, I had somewhat naively imagined he would run with me, not just sit on the park bench eating a bag of chips and shouting derogatory comments on each lap as I passed him.

"Get your arse going!"

"Knees up, fatso!"

"Show daddy your packet!"

At that moment I prayed he would be arrested for lewd conduct. After my eighth lap, I crumpled onto the bench next to him, red-faced and fighting for breath. To say I was a little unfit was unjust; I looked like a sweaty mound of Vaseline in a tracksuit. Tony tried to pop a chip in my mouth but I didn't even have enough energy to chew – highly unlike me!

Back at his, I got what I was aching for; a drink. After guzzling most of the Pepsi, Tony got what he was aching for too. He buried his face in my trainers which must have been still warm, and he stayed there for a good, long time appreciating the aroma as if it were a fine wine or a heavily scented bunch of flowers. After he was done sniffing, he peeled my socks from my cooling feet, pushed me onto the bed and got stuck in. As he let out an orgasmic moan, I echoed it with my own relaxing sigh. His tongue danced between my toes and up and down my sole, a little ticklish at first, but I had to hold my hands up and say it was absolute heaven. My poor feet had been put through their paces today – crammed into hard, new trainers and then rigorously pounded around Hyde Park, so this was a most welcome reward. I was almost falling asleep as he was climaxing into one of my trainers but I came to life when needed and made out like I was enjoying the moment as much as he was. Then he paid and I left.

Back at my flat I soaked in a hot bath until the water turned tepid. I knew I'd be as stiff as a board in the morning. As I dried my feet, the ticklish sensation made me think of Tony and I hung on the thought for a moment. Jesus, what a life!

The Strangest Proposition.

My mind was wandering in all different directions; I was in St Kilda on a gorgeous, hot, sunny day, sitting at a Fitzroy Street bistro, sipping at a skinny latté and picking at a chocolate muffin. Within an instant I was wandering the kaleidoscope streets of Harajuku late at night while the same December air now bit harshly at my ears. A world that was so far away but so real that when I breathed in I could smell buckwheat noodles as intensely as if a bowl had just been brought out to me. As the dark Japanese streets faded away, the reality of my boring date came hazily back into view.

Hugh was still droning on about his work – the very reason that I had mentally detached myself from him in the first instance and went on a whirlwind trip around the world – imagining being anywhere but there. Here was yet another dull businessman, wanting a break from his wife and his job; he had called me because he wanted to hook up for 'a little bit of fun' as he put it. If this was the extent of it, surely it was false advertising I had grounds to sue? I watched him without listening, his mouth was in overdrive; skinny pink lips that drew back to reveal a set of beautifully uniformed teeth. His eyes were darting all over the place and his hands were equally as animated: it's just a pity his story was going nowhere with them.

"….and I told him that if he wanted to try that again I would knock him flat out." He said looking heroic and weak at the same time.

"I'm sorry, what?"

Hugh looked a little confused then launched into his monologue once again. I picked at his words and realised his boss was unhappy with him and that once in the lift on the way to the canteen, Hugh was jostled by him and so picked a fight with him. I was trying to listen but I really couldn't pay any more attention. My eyes were glazing over so much they were almost opaque, and if it wasn't for the fact that I had deliberately placed my drink square in front of me, I would have let my boredom overcome me and land face down on the table with a thud.

I took a slurp of my Mojito in the hope that it would revive me somewhat, and it did for a moment until he started up again.

"Excuse me – little boy's room" I said as I slid from the table. I must have looked like I'd just woken up in the middle of the night as I steadied myself on the bar while I groggily clambered to the loo. I went into a cubicle, lowered both seats and sat on them for a few minutes, thinking of how I could end this night quickly and still get paid. Hugh definitely wasn't the wham, bam thank you ma'am type. He sure did have a tendency to make little things stretch out and because he was paying for me tonight, he was going to make it last. I checked my watch; 8:07pm. Bollocks. I looked around the cubicle and read the graffiti to pass some time. I had no idea that a great literary genius frequented this bar, for dotted on the wall just above the toilet roll holder was a poem.

As I sit here, upon my throne
I do beggin to think
That in this bog, I drop my log
And man it starts too stink

When u are hear, sat were I am
And get to reading this
Dont be a prick, just make it quick
And only take a piss

I sat for a minute contemplating that if I'd had a marker pen, I would have corrected the spelling and possibly added a third verse when I realised Hugh was still waiting for me. Reluctantly I made my way back to the table to join him, when I was stopped by a sight that would never usually stop me. I tried to avert my eyes and head back to my table but I couldn't take my eyes off her. She was totally stunning – the most beautiful woman I had ever seen in my life. Perhaps for a split second I was having a heterosexual flutter. Mother would've been so proud.

She was sitting at the bar on a stool, her amazingly long legs trailed out from under the daring split in her dress. They looked so silky and smooth and I had the strangest compulsion just to touch them. She was looking at me and her eyes were dazzling green like two neon lights shining in the dark, holding me and controlling me. Her painted mouth curled up into a sexy smile and she held out her elegant hand, clasping an unlit cigarette between two fingers, waiting for a light. Casually glancing over at Hugh, I saw he was talking on his mobile phone so I took this opportunity to be a good boy scout and offer her a light. As I approached her, I walked into a cloud of her intoxicating perfume. Instantly I was surrounded by roses, honey, vanilla and everything else sweet and beautiful I had ever smelt. I breathed in greedily. Her skin was flawless like porcelain, her hair so smooth it cascaded down from the top of her head like liquid and she had possibly the most perfect face in all living humanity. She was looking at me with strength and intensity, though her body and movements were perfectly fluid.

"Do you have a light for me?" she seemed to purr.

For a moment I was unable to speak – it was like we were the only two people in the bar. I mustered my composure and told her that I didn't. She looked a little saddened. "Perhaps – perhaps this might be a good time for you to start?" Yes, this *was* a perfect time to start. Her eyes drifted away from mine and I followed them to a bowl of matches on the bar. Slowly she turned back to look at me, waiting. As I reached out to pluck a box, she threw out a girlish laugh and I couldn't help but smile. I struck a match and held it gently to her cigarette. She cupped my hand with hers and sucked up the tiny flame, then licked her lips and softly blew out a stream of smoke, extinguishing the match at the same time. Her eyes drew me in again and quickly I was lost in their green light.

"Isn't your…friend going to wonder where you are?" she asked me. I furrowed my brow as I tried to work out who she was referring to - then I realise she meant Hugh. Damn him – why was he there?

"Oh, him? Well – he's not really a friend, but I suppose I should really get back to him."

"Yes, I suppose you should really" she repeated "but first you will let me buy you a drink – to thank you for lighting my cigarette."

"Oh, that's really not necessary at all – it was nothing – it was…a pleasure."

"Yes it was, wasn't it? But I insist. You will sit and drink with me." I was unable to refuse; her voice seemed to be imbued with a raw power.

Turning to the barman with a steely look, she signalled for a bottle and was immediately awarded with Champagne. I sat quietly, next to her, not taking my eyes from her as the barman filled two glasses for us. She didn't need to speak, she was already saying so much - I understood her completely as she played with the matchbox on the bar. Again she took a long draw on her cigarette and blew a steady steam of smoke in my direction. Somehow even the smoke she was exhaling smelt beautiful.

"What is your name, dar-ling?" she spoke like a goddess – commanding attention and respect.

"Rich. I'm very pleased to meet you…?"

"Angelina" she said, exaggerating every letter so that it sounded more like "Anshellinarr".

I glanced at Hugh who was now looking around for me, unaware that I was on a separate date all of its own. I felt bad. I felt bad for him and I felt sorry for her. I should've told her that I was busy, and even if I wasn't, that I was gay.

"I er, I really should make a move back to my…friend".

Sipping at her drink she shrugged slightly, "If you want dar-ling." I made a move to stand and before I placed even one foot on the floor she asked, "…is that what you want, dar-ling?"

I didn't know. Why was I even sitting with her? I had never in my life approached a woman like that – the nearest I had gotten to that moment was sixteen years ago at school when I approached Katie Brady and said that I would French kiss her if she let me have one of her mint humbugs. I got the sweet in the end, but I realised two things on that day: one, that I was gay; and two, that I didn't really care much for mint humbugs. Angelina sipped at her drink again, leaving her lips moist and at that sight I actually felt a surge of electricity course through me. Out of the corner of my eye I could see Hugh leave our table, make his way to the exit and disappear into the night. Now I had no reason to leave – I repositioned myself on my stool, again overcome by the sweet scent of her perfume and took another lungful.

"Are you here alone tonight?" I asked, realising the last thing I want to do is be lured into some weird sex act with Angelina and her lover if he existed. Without speaking she shook her head slowly, so that the earrings hanging from her ears sprang to life like tiny wind chimes. Her dark hair dripped over one of her eyes and without sweeping it back, she looked at me through it which I found incredibly sexy.

"No. Not anymore".

"I should tell you that I don't think I am quite what you might have been looking for, if indeed you were looking for anything tonight at all, that is." I offered lamely. It didn't faze her.

"I know you aren't, but I find you…out of the ordinary, someone very…motivating." She chose each word and pronounced it with such purpose, like she had just discovered the ability to use simple words to control people around her. I swelled with pride – I had never been described as out of the ordinary before, and I liked it.

"You too" I reply. "I think you are exceptional. Of course, I'm sure you know I'm gay. But somehow, that doesn't seem to matter. Who are you?"

Again she let out a coquettish laugh and placed her hand upon mine.

"I am your lucky night" she whispers. "Tell me, that man you were here with – who was he?"

Flushing with colour, I tried to figure out if I should let her know the truth or spin some old yarn. I hated lying, but given the type of work I did it came quite easily. She drained her glass and eyed the barman who seemed to also to be captivated by her and immediately he began to refill her glass.

"He was one of my clients. I'm a...." not knowing how to finish, I paused. Re-assessing the situation I was in, I let my imagination grip me tightly and decided to throw myself into it all and see where it got me. "I'm a gigolo" I declared with a half smile, and knocked back my drink in one go. She turned to me and her eyes seemed to burn with delight. "Didn't I say you were out of the ordinary? I knew it. Intrigue, imagination, inspiration – you are interesting dar-ling! And you have given me the most wonderful idea!" she said, while gesturing the barman to top up my drink.

The champagne bottle emptied quickly and another one was put in its place. Minutes turned to hours with lightening speed but it felt like Angelina and I had been talking for the shortest time. I had never really had amazing sex with anyone that I really cared for, shagging clients was fun and I learnt many new things which made me a well seasoned lover, but that aside, sex has always been just that little bit empty - to me it was a bit like Christmas; very exciting when you were planning it but when it was actually happening, you just wanted it to be done with so you could do something more productive. But sitting here with Angelina, I knew what was coming and this would have to be the strangest proposition I would ever have.

We moved to a booth as it was more comfortable – more private and more seductive; I was more than happy to be seduced. Angelina rested her hand just above my knee and was laughing heartily in response to a joke I had just made. With each mouthful of champagne, the taste was becoming more and more pleasurable, sweeter and sweeter, and with each of these little seductions I was getting drunker and drunker. Angelina seemed to have a resistance to it - if she was as drunk as I was, she was hiding it well. She moved her face so close to mine that I could feel her breath dance over my cheek. "Shall we leave my darling?"

I laughed a silly laugh. "Where are you taking me now?" I asked presumptuously.

"I have a car outside. Come with me, you won't regret it". I believed her.

The next thing I knew, I was in the dark of night with the cool air billowing around my drunkenness. She led me over to a canary-yellow Lamborghini which was so low to the ground I wondered how I would manoeuvre myself into it. Angelina had little trouble navigating her way gracefully into the seat, peering up at me, almost swallowed up by the leather interior. When I fell back into the chair, the door clicked shut and the headlights glared to full beam, just like her eyes. The engine geared up and we rocketed away from the kerb. When the car came to a halt outside her Kensington apartment, she pulled me close and kissed me severely. The taste of a woman's mouth was foreign to me and woven with the waxy taste of her lipstick. When she released me I could smell her all over me and wanted more. Outwardly I wanted to take her to her bed and make love to her, but inwardly I had a nagging worry that I wouldn't be able to perform. I had never been with a woman, what if nothing happened? What if I got stage fright?

The champagne still filled my head, but I was able to see through the fogginess and take back some control of myself. I had to pretend she was a man. I had to pretend she was the most handsome man I had ever seen and imagine that when we kissed there was no waxy lipstick or sweet smelling perfume. Most of all I had to imagine I was working. That was the reason I absent-mindedly spat out "Two hundred – for the night!"

Angelina, half out of her seat, stopped and slowly sank back. Shit – I had blown it. I had insulted her beyond belief and now it was off. To offer a woman I had never met before sex for money – surely I would be feeling the lash of her hand across my face at any moment. We sat in silence, just eyeing each other.

"Dar-ling – you have to price yourself a little higher if you wish to get anywhere with your life - two-hundred pounds? I think we can do a little better than that?"

For the second time that evening I was unable to speak; only barely managing to choke out the word "Th-three?"

"Five!" she said defiantly, and with this she removed herself from the vehicle and I quickly followed.

I followed her into her apartment; watching her walk in front of me was hypnotic. As the key in the lock turned, so did Angelina, casting me a very cheeky smile.

As I crossed the threshold, I beheld her sanctuary. I had never known a woman to have such similar tastes as myself. Beautiful original floor boards adorned the apartment, their telltale knotholes untouched after years of the renovation that had been undertaken on the rest of the house. There was a slight polish on them but nothing too garish. Typical of the old Kensington houses, the height of the ceilings in each of the rooms was vast.

She strode down to the kitchen at the end of the main hall and pointed for me to take a seat in the lounge room. As I entered I spotted an unpretentious and artistic arrangement of furniture - the type that a cultured person would own; not having to rely on showy pieces to communicate sophistication.

I took a seat on the cream, hard-backed leather sofa and was looking around the room as Angelina's heels clacked down the hall, rounding into the lounge room with a bucket of ice and another bottle of champagne.

We sat on the sofa together under the harsh gallery-style lighting overhead. She removed her gown and sat on the huge sofa in only her underwear, which seemed to hold onto her body so tightly it was almost trying to squeeze her out of it. Reaching across the table she pulled a silver tray toward her with a mound of white powder piled in the middle. Using a knife that lay on the tray, she cut a small line and wasted no time in sniffing it up, then sat back on the sofa with closed eyes, still inhaling with the look of a child breathing in the air of a patisserie. Then it happened. She reached behind herself and unhooked her bra, letting it fall away from her body. I wasn't too sure as I had never been so close to a half-naked woman before, but it appeared she had perfect breasts. I wanted to cup them and squeeze them, but found myself standing on ceremony and not knowing if it was polite to ask before squeezing a lady's bosom. I myself was half-dressed without realising how I had become so. My shirt had been flung into a corner of the room and my belt and trousers were undone at the waist.

I cannot say how long it lasted, but while it went on I was lost in some of the most adventurous sex I had ever taken part in. The comparison between man and woman was vivid. Here it was so tended to and so prepared, while a majority of the sex I had with men was so uncultivated. She was passionate and fiery, but never lost her style. Her body entwined around mine and her lips danced all over my body, me barely knowing what to do. I let her guide me as I tried things that I never thought I'd be doing. I pleasured her as best I could and hoped it was enough. Soon enough though my natural abilities shined through and I took control. While buried between her legs and tasting new flavours, she arched her back and let out a guttural moan – clearly I was good at this. Why were straight men so hopeless at finding a woman's sensitive areas? Being a gigolo, I was armed with a good sense of direction and tailored my efforts accordingly.

I was amazed at how light she was. I picked her up and pressed her against the wall as I buried my face in her neck, kissing and nuzzling her as her legs wrapped around me. The rest came naturally as we moved around the room trying out different things, sharing and laughing together as we both completely lost any inhibitions.

I awoke in an empty bed; sunlight charging into the room through the full-length windows, tearing me from my dream. I glanced at a clock on the bedside table – it was eleven.

"Good morning my dar-ling". Angelina was dressed in a silk kimono and as she walked toward the bed, dragons danced all around her.

Without her make-up, she was naturally beautiful, her cheeks were glowing and her eyes still dazzled. She placed a tray upon the bed next to me. "I will have to ask you to leave soon – I have a lunch date with a professor, and I simply cannot be late, I hope you don't mind?" She then vanished into the en-suite bathroom and the shower roared to life.

On the tray was a cappuccino in an oversized cup, complete with chocolate sprinkles and a generous serving of biscotti. Next to the cup was a bulging envelope. As I lifted the seal, a series of £20 notes peeped out at me. My heart skipped a beat for a moment. Five hundred pounds! I remembered from last night, she wasn't joking. I drained my cappuccino and scoffed the biscotti which seemed to quell the growling in my stomach. The shower had died down as I began to dress, and I tucked the envelope into my inside pocket.

Angelina stepped out of the bathroom wearing a tiny towel, her body still beaded with water.

"You don't mind if I don't show you out do you? I have to get ready for my appointment. Just pull the door to – it will lock itself."

I tapped my pocket and thanked her.

"Thank *you*" she said through her smile.

The door closed behind me with a click and I walked out into the world, not caring in which direction I was going. I would hail a taxi home – I was able to afford the fare, whatever it may be. Thinking back on the night I had to smile.

It was an unusual evening, and although now I had achieved something that I could cross off my list of things to do before I die, I was happy in my self and the lifestyle that I had chosen (or had chosen me).

I pulled out my mobile phone; six missed calls and three texts. Ignoring them, I pulled up Juan's number and began to type.

'Ur never going 2 believe wot happened 2 me last night!'

In a black cab somewhere by Hyde Park Corner, 11pm.

Juan was cackling to the caller on his mobile phone while playing with his huge visor sunglasses that swallowed his entire forehead. It was not out of place for him to wear such an item while out shopping in Chelsea or mincing around Portobello Road, but rarely did he rely on them for a night out. Truth be told, he'd had a little accident earlier as I was waiting for him at his flat while he got ready. I was in the living room pawing through various CDs and glugging from my large glass of red wine while he was in his bedroom layering the *Touche Eclat* to his entire face. Just as I was about to pop The Cranberries on, he screeched loudly.

"Rich. I've done something bad!" he half sobbed.

Of course I shouted in to him but he was silent. I shouted again. This time his response was panic ridden.

"I've – I've had an...accident! Tell me the truth, oh Rich, please tell me it's not too bad!" I swallowed a large gulp of wine and headed to his room which was rife with a combination of several expensive fragrances. When I approached him, his back was turned and upon hearing me he slowly turned on his heels, one hand clasped to the left side of his face in terror. After a few seconds, he lowered his hand from his face and I saw what he had done. It took every single muscle in my body to prevent myself exploding into a fit of laughter.

"I...I noticed my eyebrows were getting a bit bushy. I just wanted a little trim, you know, tidy up the area - that Brazilian girl I usually see didn't do it last time and I thought to myself, well, it's only a razor. But I've fucked up the smallest thing. Is it bad?"

I clenched my mouth shut so that my lips must have been turning white. I shook my head slowly, daring not to let the built-up laughter escape from me. While getting a little over-zealous with the electric razor, he had decided to define the track line in his left eyebrow, but hadn't quite achieved the look he wanted. In actual fact, he had shorn away over half of it, leaving only a centimetre of hair left sitting above his watery eye. To add insult to injury, where he had applied coat after coat of fake tan, the space, which moments before was occupied by an eyebrow, was now just a thin, pink patch.

At that moment the taxi beeped for us and Juan erupted in screams of panic. Simply not going out wasn't even an option - he had paid over two hundred pounds for these tickets and he was going to get his money's worth. Reaching for the largest pair of sunglasses from a box of about ten, he slapped them to his face and near dragged me out, leaving The Cranberries to party all by themselves in his empty flat.

"No! I swear on my mother's life – she did. She did! All the way in! I know – I know, that's what I said! Uh huh? Uh huh? Well, honey, let me tell you what I heard….uh huh? Yeah – too right! I know – like waving a twig in the Thames" and Juan creased up into salacious laughter. "Ok honey, yeah, ok then, I'll call you soon, ok? You be good now. Uh huh? And I want *all* the details, dirty bitch! Ciao!!" Snapping his phone shut, he swivelled on his seat to pick up our conversation.

"So, who was she?"

"I don't know – she was just…" I stumbled, not even knowing where to start. I was still having trouble dealing with the whole situation, mostly how easy and enjoyable the whole experience had been.

Juan he cut me off, cupping at imaginary breasts "You slept with a woman! Oh my *God!*" he screeched so loud, the cab driver looked in his rear view mirror to check we were both ok.

It had been a week and a half since my female conquest and Juan had safely returned to the UK, looking a very healthy shade of chestnut. Before I could respond, he continued "Well you are something else. But hey – good on you! I am so…well, honey, I ain't jealous – but you did good." I felt myself swell with pride a little as he spoke these words – it was not often one managed to prise a compliment from his glossy lips, so to be hearing this now was a good thing.

"Here please, right here darling" he squealed to the taxi driver. The door opened and we stepped out into the blackened night. As I was shivering slightly in the wind, Juan was pressing a twenty into the cabby's hand.

"Keep the change darling – ciao!"

The muffled music made its way out of the entrance to *El Tempo* and reverberated into the night. A mix of cool trip-hop and sexy Latin beats were enticing us in just as much as the rush of warm air that seemed to circle around us as we blitzed past the queue. Once inside, I could hardly hear a word he was saying; he could have been singing for all I knew. My suspicions were confirmed when he flung his coat to the poor doorman and began gyrating about and rubbing himself up the wall like a deranged pole dancer. I figured this was a good time to make my way to the bar.

The club was amazing; unlike any place I'd ever been to before. Juan was right – it was *the* place to be. A giant, red, satin swag hung from the stupendously high ceiling, pinned in all corners and in the centre, giving the feeling one was in a lavishly over-decorated tent. Chandeliers dripped from the ceiling and sprinkled their diffused light over a pumping dance floor. Shirtless bodies bounded around to the music while couples on the dance floor embraced and flung each other around, stopping every few minutes to lock in passionate kisses. Among the crowd of happy clubbers were such treats as fire-eaters spitting flames high into the air and gorgeous caged boys, wearing next to nothing; seemingly clawing to get out on the dance floor to release their pent-up energy. It was a visual explosion of colour and while Juan had launched into the midst of revellers on the dance floor, I was happy to settle into one of the squishy chairs on the mezzanine, happily slurping on a gin and tonic. As I sat watching, I noticed how much I was getting checked out from both guys on the dance floor and the ones strutting past me toward the bar - it was like tonight was the last night on earth and everyone was destined to hook up. I played my game coolly, smirking here and there to a baying crowd of Latin beauties, pretty-looking rough boys and handsome preppy lads. I loved this club!

After an hour or so, I was spinning around on the dance floor, lost in the beat with my bevy of beauties around me. I spotted Juan who was seated at a table up on the mezzanine and he was holding court to two very fit looking men indeed. The air in the club was hot and clingy and my shirt was damp all over from my sweat. I must have looked hot, for as I danced, a pair of strange hands began undoing the buttons on my shirt. In a second, it was ripped from my body and thrown into the music. I threw my head back and shouted happily, but my noise was lost among the party. While I danced, I had the feeling someone was behind me very close – we were dancing back to back. Gently our bodies touched and released as I felt a cool tingle through the heat of my skin. Keeping casual and controlled I carried on dancing, not daring to turn around, and hoping to keep the mystery alive. The hands from my new dancing partner reached out to my thigh from behind so I decided to shimmy down, letting his hands climb my body. He returned the favour as I put my hands down to my sides and then behind me. Then he must have turned around and was now standing so close behind me, dancing with me, that I could feel the heat from his body and his breath on my neck. His hands reached around my waist this time and drew me closer, swallowing the tiny gap that was keeping us apart. Gently he caressed my torso before reaching his hands up under my arms and pulling them up behind his head, lifting my arms high up with them. I had to turn round – I couldn't take the suspense any longer. Spinning around, everything went to a blur and stopped with a sudden jolt as I found myself staring into Dylan's eyes. He looked equally as shocked as I did and we both stood there motionless among a heaving dance floor, staring in disbelief. It had been over a month since this guy had stood me up. After feeling totally rejected for weeks, I was only just getting some order back to my life – until now.

I threw my ticket to the well-dressed gentleman behind the coat check and barked for my coat before storming out into the harsh, cold dawn air.

"Hey! Wait! " I heard from behind me.

I carried on walking, trying to find a cab.

"Please, wait – I can explain." His voice sounded borderline desperate.

I spun round to look at him, wanting to say something but unable to speak, so I spun back round and carried on walking.

"I'm sorry you waited for me and I wasn't there, but it wasn't my fault...well, it was, but it's not what you think. I tried to track you down....but I don't...I don't even know your name..." he trailed off.

This time I stopped and without turning I spoke out. "Rich." I paused slightly, my defences well and truly down "My name is Rich."

Dylan caught up with me, walked around to face me and I looked into his perfect eyes. The streetlights over my shoulder illuminated him perfectly.

A good part of me wanted to make a big scene and storm off into the night, punishing him for making me feel like shit. However, a greater part of me was helpless against such a charming smile, and I decided what the hell.

"Please Rich – I'm really, really sorry – can we go somewhere and talk? At least give me a chance to explain." I couldn't help but smile, even though he had angered me so much when I was sat by myself in Rubicon. I felt a little bad for storming off when I saw him - the least I could do was listen. Plus I was kind of horny and we'd both been drinking - a bit of a fumble was also on the forefront of my mind.

"It's almost 4am. Where will we go?" I said looking at my watch.

Dylan smiled "There's an all-night café that I know around here."

As we started to walk, the cold of night suddenly ran through me – my shirtless body felt like it was iced over and I struggled with the zipper on my coat with my cold hands. Dylan took that moment to shield me from the cold, zipping me up and resting his arm around my shoulders as we walked the rest of the way.

Soon enough I was rewarded with hot coffee and food. My eggs were fabulous - maybe I was still a little hammered, but I decided then and there to ensure I was at least half-tanked the next time I made a fried egg sandwich.

Dylan explained the whole thing to me as I chomped away and when I heard his reason for unintentionally standing me up, I felt almost embarrassed.

He explained that on the fateful lunch day, just after 1pm, he jumped off the back of the bus, almost killing himself, and ran down the length of Old Compton Street dodging the daytime gays in the vain hope I would still be waiting at Rubicon. He had left his house at 11 that morning and had decided to get a professional wet shave at the barbers before meeting me because he wanted to look good. I almost choked on my crusts as he said that – he could have arrived dressed in a shit-stained sack with seven-day stubble and he'd still look hot – in a messed up, romantic heroic kind of way.

It turned out that during the shave, the barber accidentally nicked his top lip with the razor, giving him a lip haemorrhage situation with a resulting faint red moustache. He wasn't too worried as he had plenty of time to go to the chemist to get something to calm the bleeding a bit. However; while in Boots, he was understandably distracted by the fragrance section. Thinking he should squirt himself to smell good for me, he picked up a lovely bottle of something by David Beckham which somehow slipped from his grip and was heading to the ground. Luckily Dylan's reflexes were hot and he caught it before it exploded on the floor. Unluckily however, he caught it right on the nozzle, and as he gripped it, he sent a fine jet of the aftershave into one of his eyes, leaving him temporarily blinded.

With his top lip oozing blood and his left eye sealed shut in pain, he frantically reached into a nearby customer's basket and unscrewed a bottle of mineral water, drenching his face to soothe the sting. Wet, in pain and generally looking worse for wear, he bumbled his way into the street. Managing to glance at his watch with his good eye he realised he was now running late. As he was about to hop on another bus, he found himself outside a Tesco Metro and right by the fresh flower buckets. He plucked a bouquet of something pretty and headed to the till to pay – a gesture to me for arriving late. However, once inside the store, security took one look at him and thought he was up to no good, so they got him to one side and led him to a room out the back.

My fried egg sandwich was cold when I next went to bite into it, so I sipped at my coffee instead – enthralled at his story.

He said he remained calm and rational when being interrogated in Tesco, but somehow I think he was just smoothing that part over. He said he explained to security the series of unfortunate events that had happened to him and they let him go peacefully on his way. However, when he regurgitated words like "almost fucking blinded myself in Boots" and "lost three pints of blood while Freddie fucking Krueger gave me a shave" I thought he had probably been a bit more to the point with them as he was with me.

Anyway, there was no time for him to get the flowers, so he threw them at a cashier, left the store and flung himself on any available bus that was passing. After going entirely the wrong way and having to sit in road works for ten minutes, he then had to run all the way back and still get to Rubicon. He finally arrived at the restaurant damp, red-lipped, out of breath and angry to find it was 1pm and I was gone.

I was lost for words – Dylan was my milk tray man! A little part of me still wanted to be angry and stand my ground, but how could I not forgive him after hearing all that? Well simple – just as I was about to forgive him, I had a vivid flash back of Dylan and his 'friend' in the supermarket. My fists clenched under the table and I was back to being angry.

"Well, I'm sorry. I had no idea – I just thought you stood me up. It didn't bother me though" I added, lying through my teeth. "I had a fabulous afternoon; I had the most marvellous food, drinks galore and stimulating conversation" I smiled, hoping to make him jealous of me for a change. Of course, I didn't exactly tell him the truth that my lunch consisted of over-priced bruschetta, 4 drinks in 49 minutes and a verbal assault on the waiting staff.

Now that I was feeling a little bolder, I had to ask the question "But I would just like to know one thing...tha.." but before I could finish, he intervened.

"I know, I know – who was the old fart in the supermarket right?" I nodded slowly. Dylan inhaled deeply and held onto it before releasing it in a hefty blow and then broke into a very nervous laugh.

"Well, what can I say, um..., this isn't going to be easy at all and you're probably...no, there is no doubt about it. You are going to be very pissed off when you hear this. The good news is he is not my boyfriend! No way! Never has been, never ever going to be – no way".

I'm not sure if this made me feel good or bad. If they weren't going out together, surely he was banging him for some reason? I refused to believe he was just doing his good Boy Scout chores and helping the aged.

"Rich – what I'm about to tell you may really come as a shock – in fact, there's no two ways about it – it *is* going to come to you as a shock."

By this point I wanted to shake it out of him and scream *Just tell me!!*

Admittedly, I was knocked for six, but at the same time I couldn't do anything but laugh when he had explained to me that he was actually an escort.

He was very diplomatic and careful in his explanation. He said that he didn't have many friends at school and after leaving he went to college to study architecture. Soon after he started, he met a guy called Nathan who got him into some very bad habits. Because Dylan was a handsome lad, he found that he didn't have to rely on his brain too often as his looks got him most places. Then he fell in with a group of guys who exploited him and made him use his looks and his body to get further ahead. Struggling for money as he was, he did what they suggested and as soon as he saw how much money he could get by selling himself, he just became accustomed to that. One thing led to another and there you have it; one easy recipe for a home-made rent boy.

Dylan returned to my question after giving me his background. It transpired that the old guy in the supermarket was one of his best clients, and was staying with him while his flat was being redecorated. Dylan explained that he no longer sees him since a colonic went wrong, adding that pushing him around in a wheelchair in bars became too embarrassing, and that his reputation was worth more than what he earned from him anyway.

I ordered us two more strong black coffees as he then asked me about how I got involved in escorting. I launched into my early days of my career and how I met Juan. I also told him of my time at school and how I had always felt like an outsider in my life until I met Juan and thought I'd found my place in life.

At first, he was lost for words; amazed that we both had a pretty similar but rubbish school life. In a way, it was almost perfect that we were so similar - for me, it was a great healing process to be able to talk to someone who had gone on such a similar journey.

For the next hour Dylan and I grilled each other about our clients; who were they, did we know each other's, what were the funnier experiences, the usual rent-boy-to-rent-boy conversation really. Luckily it seemed that Dylan only met normal people who paid him for sex and that was it. Turns out all the freaks had sunk their claws into me and didn't need to stray anywhere else. Dylan laughed uproariously as I told him some of the highlights of my time so far – hiding in a closet, having to deal with Tony Tonsils, being busted by Miles in his study. Strangely enough, his response to my encounter with Angelina was very different from Juan's. He asked me what it was like, how it felt. Perhaps we all have a little curiosity in us somewhere – I didn't realise that I was able to explore new frontiers and share it with a large audience.

As we finished sharing stories of our clients, I quizzed him quite candidly about his availability in life. I probably shouldn't have done it, but I didn't want to have any wrong expectations about what my next step would be. If he was hooked up with someone and madly in love, I wanted to know about it. If he was in a long term relationship, but taking a break from his childhood sweetheart, then I wanted to know about it. I wanted to know about everything – I had to find out if he had baggage; too many times I had fallen for the guy who wasn't available and it hurt. There were only so many times you could get your heart kicked, so this time I wasn't taking any chances.

He assured me he was single, totally single and only ever been in one relationship – exactly the same as myself. As we chatted, it became more than evident we both liked each other a lot and we actually had a lot in common – well, a lot more than we had initially bargained for. I was happy – the moment I had hung on to for ages was here and I wasn't sure if I was dreaming it.

Outside, the sun had risen in the sky and it was a beautifully warm Sunday morning. We had been chatting and eating for almost four hours, but time meant nothing while we were together. I liked the way he laughed and the way he always seemed to close his eyes when laughing at my bad jokes. I also liked the way that when he spoke, he stole little glances at me for a fleeting second before pretending he hadn't. I couldn't believe we were finally spending time together since our first real meeting all those weeks ago in Sainsbury's.

After swapping numbers, we reluctantly parted and headed to our homes for some rest and a lazy Sunday. As I turned the corner onto the high street, only a few feet from where we said goodbye, I got a text message. It was from Dylan.

'Miss u already, toilet roll man.'

Somewhere in a state of bliss.

It had been officially three weeks since I'd bagged myself a real boyfriend and I couldn't stop myself from gloating. I was starting to view things differently and appreciated life in a different way now that I was in a relationship, and this morning I had been looking through the Argos catalogue looking at things I could buy that no single person would ever want. So far I had contemplated buying a tea making machine with two cups, perfect for lazy mornings in bed together, a pair of matching wedding bands from the Elizabeth Duke section (not that I would ever really buy them), and I had made a mental list of all the birthday-type gifts I would buy him from the 'gifts for him' pages.

Since our first date we had been pretty much inseparable. I dreaded to think what my phone bill was going to be but I guessed that was just one of the things I had to put up with once I entered into a real relationship. Ah, just saying those words made me feel as light as a feather. I would not, however, become totally consumed by it and would endeavour to maintain a sense of self awareness and a sense of individuality. Ooh, Argos had a special offer on matching bathrobes.

Last week he wanted to take me for a romantic weekend away, or that was his intention. Due to unforeseen work commitments (more him than me) this became a romantic afternoon out. He picked me up in his little blue Fiat and we had a lovely drive to the coast. It was amazing and I had to berate myself for worrying about the drive there and what we would talk about. Truth was you couldn't shut us up. It was like we had grown up together or something, we clicked beyond clicking. We had so much in common and as conversationalists went, we were up there with the best. It was a perfect afternoon, the weather was glorious and when we arrived, Dylan had prepared a picnic for us both. We sat out over-looking the sea just feeding each other, laughing and sharing a bottle of wine, even though I drank most of it due to the fact he still had to get us home.

Then there was the house party we went to together on the weekend. As a rule of thumb, I tend not to go to them too often as I don't generally like them. Guests tend to get a bit too carried away and before you knew it there was vomit on the bed spread and someone had made off with the Shania Twain CD. But it wasn't my house or my party so I went because he wanted me to go. We had a great night until someone passed around a joint. Dylan took a long drag on it and sank back into his chair relaxing. Weed doesn't have the best effect on me but I didn't want to appear boring so I too took a long drag. I couldn't be sure if it was the wine, the lager, the gin or the joint, but something compelled me to rush upstairs looking for the bathroom. I don't think I found it because Dylan woke me up in the early hours of the morning and scooped me off of the vomit-stained bedspread to take me home.

And just two nights ago I invited him over for a lovely home cooked meal. I didn't do too badly, having gotten over my nervousness around him, I was actually focused and managed to pull off a great meal. Dylan was wrapped at having someone take the time to cook for him. We had a wonderful night, the food was good and the wine was better.

We chatted about all sorts of stuff, but his eyes really lit up when I mentioned travelling – it appeared he had a keen interest for it. I liked to travel as well, but I hadn't been to many places, whereas he had trekked quite far. He told me some of the fantastic places he had been and the wonderful stories that came with it – I was a little green-eyed but happy to be sharing them with him.

Without directly saying it, he spoke about how we would share some amazing stories one day in some amazing country. Then when he caught on to what he was saying I think it worried him that he might be freaking me out so he just stopped talking. I wasn't freaked out at all – since meeting him I had already been drifting on into daydreams that saw us together in the future. I was finding it hard to believe that I had met him, guys like this didn't normally exist did they? And if they did, why did they like me?

Dylan and I decided that we wouldn't rush into the sexual side of our relationship. It was a little ironic, and Juan nearly died laughing when I told him, but it felt right. I didn't want to view him as some sort of conquest to be made, or treat him the same as I treated my clients – this was the real deal and we were both happy waiting until the time was right.

I had to say, the greatest thing about my fabulous relationship, aside from the smug feeling of finding someone who wanted me was even when we weren't together, was that we were both thought about each other a lot. Debs told me on the phone a few nights back that if she heard the words 'Dylan, relationship or happy' once more she would hang up. I must say, I was lost in my own world with him, even clients didn't faze me. I was giving them the best servicing of their lives probably, I was on such a high nothing was getting to me.

I had finally traded in my provisional dating license and was now the proud owner of a happy relationship permit.

My Refrigerator - Third Shelf.

Bag of lettuce: keep.

Leftover Chinese from Thursday: definitely throw.

Mayonnaise (97% fat free): keep.

Strawberry Jam with real fruit pieces: keep. No, I mustn't. Throw.

Tesco mini éclairs: Well, as I was officially starting my health kick tomorrow, I should dispose of them now.

Pulling my sticky fingers from my over-stuffed mouth, I continued to hunt through the fridge looking for anything unhealthy that I should be throwing out or finishing. I had to say that this was a new experience for me, never before had I been overly concerned with my weight. In fact, I was always the one who sat at the dinner table eating until I felt sick and then, more often than not, eating more, proudly shouting to the rest of the table (usually through a mouthful of food) that I could eat as much as I wanted and never gain a pound. It turned out the pounds had finally caught up with me and were charging me interest in arrears from 1997. I hadn't even noticed - I was quite happy riding along in life, completely oblivious to calories, fat, carbs and all things diet. I'd never really cared for healthy options as I knew my body would process anything I ate and leave me with quite the trim figure.

I was alerted to the fact that I was fast approaching Blue Whale status when last night's client had asked me to stop halfway through sex. It was all fine when we first started and were making out on his bed. However, things got rapidly worse from there. I noticed that he wasn't really touching me and let me do all the work. Usually I'm fine with that – however when I asked him beforehand what turned him on, he was saying that lots of caressing and touching were his weaknesses. It all came to a head when he was on his back with his legs on my shoulders. I was doing what I do best, working away like a trouper when he pulled the plug on the show, because apparently, looking up at me sweating away and puffing like an old man had caused him to lose the mood.

I decided then and there that I needed to get my body back into shape. Actually, to be honest, it was when I was standing outside his door with a reduced fee in my hand ("why should I pay you the whole amount when you couldn't make me cum?") that I made my decision.

I had woken up this morning at six o'clock and tidied my flat in preparation for the day. Today was the day I would turn myself around. I had started off by staring at myself long and hard in the mirror to see what I needed to fix. I wouldn't say I was fat, but the fact that I could now squeeze two rolls of fat on my belly together to make a gigantic mouth and perform a decent ventriloquist show did not give me a great sense of encouragement. I was hoping that I could just lift a few weights or perhaps run to the fridge rather than walk and I would be okay. It looked like I was going to need to go through urban renewal to get this body back on track.

I decided to dedicate the day to plan a new routine for myself. I needed to do something today other than sit and text Dylan. It had only been a couple of weeks since we swapped numbers and given how hard it was to coordinate time together, we've been making up for it by texting each other like it was going out of fashion. Rather than jumping in head-first on the exercise and salad regime, I decided that I would create a plan, and for most of the morning I had been on the computer creating a suite of health-related spreadsheets. I had a spreadsheet detailing food intake, one for exercise requirements and I even had one for my moods (so I could gauge what set of exercises and food groups would illicit the best emotional responses). This really was terribly professional of me. The spreadsheets occupied the entire front of my fridge, leaving no room for any of the dirty postcards from Juan or novelty magnets that had found their way into my home, courtesy of some random relative.

I had also started a list of words that I would banish from my vocabulary; Fat, Éclair, Bacon, Alcohol (except vodka and maybe the odd glass of Sauv Blanc), Häagen-Dazs (or any type of ice cream really), buffet, Nutella, Pizza Hut/KFC/Maccy D's/Lucky Dragon over the road/Bombay House next door to Lucky Dragon – in fact all fast food and takeaways. Ooh, except sushi. I figured that if I didn't even mention these words, they wouldn't associate themselves with me, keeping myself skinny and fit and enabling me to stare blankly at people when they use the name of any of the fast food names which I adored: out of mind, out of stomach.

The great fridge/cupboard cleanout was the last thing on my day's agenda. If I had done it first, I would have most likely spent the rest of the day depressed and pining for something that would have been in the bin. Sorting my day this way ensured I had inspired myself with my spreadsheet organisation; now it was a great exercise in reconciling my day by emptying out the things that had made me…less slim. Right at the back of the fridge I found a tub of cream from when I made that homemade sponge-cake which was for Debs' 28th birthday. Given that she's now in her thirties, I gingerly picked it up and placed it in the bin so I didn't accidentally pop the lid and gas myself to death.

Tomorrow would be the start of the new Rich Harrison.

The New Rich - Day 1.

11am update:

Breakfast: One toasted bagel with nothing on it, one large glass of low GI fruit juice, one tub of yoghurt and one apple

Exercise: Two-mile run around Holland Park

Mood: Motivated and Happy

Number of texts to/from Dylan since waking: a normal 4

After an ambitious run around Holland Park, I had seen eight hot guys, and five not-so-hot-but-still-fuckable ones. I thought the whole exercise thing was a great idea, why hadn't I thought about it before; it was a great way to meet men.

To prepare me for my new fitness regime, I had splurged out and bought myself a hot little athletic sleeveless running top and some cute shorts. It was only a matter of time before I bagged myself a husband and lived happily ever after, both of us running hand in hand through the parks of Greater London together. After I'd had a quick breather on a bench, looking back proudly at the distance I had covered, I decided to head back home to my apartment. I couldn't help but feel very satisfied with myself and sensed the people around me were staring, probably with envious eyes while they lived out their fat-indulgent and ugly existences. That's right people; feast your eyes on the model of healthy living.

After my morning run, I decided to treat myself to a spot of window shopping on Kensington High Street, after all, it was within my best interest to thoroughly cool down after such rigorous exercise. Stopping outside French Connection and looking in at the new season's fashion;

I gazed longingly through the window into the store. I was the worst impulse buyer; I just couldn't help but buy the first thing that I fell in love with. As I daydreamed on, I saw a fabulous pair of jeans that were slightly ripped and faded, almost to the point that they looked really retro and very eighties. I wanted them – I wanted them because I knew they would make me look young and funky, and I drooled at the very thought of stepping into them. Considering it another type of exercise, I allowed myself to enter the store, just to try them on – all that stepping and bending had to be good for me – and I definitely wouldn't buy them. Thinking for a moment I realised that even if I was going to, I couldn't – I had hardly any cash with me and had purposely left my credit card at home – I'd revised this healthy, new lifestyle to also include debt loss.

As I was about to jog into the shop, (my attempt at a pre-warm up for trying them on), I heard a polite cough from behind me and turned around and see Tony Tonsils standing before me.

"Tony. Hi, er - how are you?" I smiled unconvincingly.

"'allo stranger, where've you been then? I've left messages on your phone" he said, looking me up and down as he was talking.

"Oh well, you know me Tony, I get far too many calls from…people like you, sometimes I just lose track" I said, stumbling for some sort of excuse. I looked down at his trousers, knowing that the sight of me in my sweaty runners was already giving him a raging stiffy.

"Really, you get so many calls from men wanting to lick in between your toes and have you rub their ball sack with the sole of your foot? You must give me their names!" he said sarcastically. "Just been for a run?

You look really good, you know…sweaty. You working today?" he leered at me, his disgusting breath overpowering the smell of the traffic and the unwashed miscreants begging nearby.

"Oh…erm, no. In fact, I was thinking about knocking it on the head for a bit - you know – start a clean slate" I lied, again probably quite unconvincingly.

"Yeah, yeah, whatever, I wouldn't be so quick to dismiss potential offers if I were you. I've just been to the bank as a matter of fact and I'm feeling rather charitable". Moving closer to me he whispered into my ear, "Come around behind that church with me and let me smell your socks. Then after I wanna suck your feet clean!" My eyes were actually beginning to sting - he smelt worse than a cadaver. As I was about to decline and run away, I remembered those beautiful jeans in the shop. "Fine" I said "I'll give you half an hour".

I looked on the bright side as I walked out of FCUK three quarters of an hour later with my new jeans. Exercising was not only helping me lose weight, it was earning me money too. If I was really lucky, maybe I could bankrupt Tony on my way to healthy living.

3pm update:
Lunch: Sashimi salad and one vegetable hand roll from local sushi restaurant
Exercise: Brisk walk around streets
Mood: Glad to be alive
Number of texts I've sent to Dylan since 11am: a psychotic 17

Debs and Jacqui had dropped by to hang out for the afternoon and thankfully they hadn't brought any of their ugly, single gay friends with, so were actually able to have a satisfying, uninterrupted catch-up session. Jacqui had a couple of bottles of wine under her arm and she pushed past me into my apartment with a kiss on the cheek, and headed straight for the kitchen. I politely turned down the offer of a glass, instead swigging from my Evian bottle instead. Both girls rolled their eyes at each other, Jacqui exclaiming "Well, never mind – more for us Debs!"

We were sitting on the balcony out the back, looking over the road into the private gardens that I shared with my neighbours; otherwise known as the upper-crust wankers. Two children were running around while their parents were setting up a picnic blanket underneath one of the large elms. Debs, Jacqui and I spent a good hour catching up over what we'd all been up to since the three of us were last together. Jacqui had been out of town for two weeks talking at workshops around the country, so it had been ages since we'd all seen each other. I was careful to let a healthy amount of conversation take place before I gave them my update about Dylan. Jacqui was really excited about it all, asking me for details and giggling with delight as I told her how we were reacquainted at El Tempo. However, I got the sense that Debs, although accepting of Dylan's excuse for standing me up (she was the one who had to pick up the pieces when I was crushed), still had her reservations.

"Just don't jump in head first" she cautioned me. I rolled my eyes, but part of me knew that she was only trying to keep me from flying off into the sunset with my expectations. "It's only been what, a month?"

"Okay, okay" I cut her off, and then smiled at her to show that I understood where she was coming from and she had no need to worry.

"What's he like in bed?" Jacqui casually asked me. I didn't know how to answer, as I was actually quite embarrassed.

"Um...well...I kind of don't know...yet" I mumbled. Both the girls shrieked at once, laughing and asking me to clarify what I had just said.

"But you're gigolos, escorts; whore-bags if you will" cackled Debs "how the hell can you not have slept with each other yet?" Obviously they thought it was the funniest thing they had ever heard while was left feeling a little bit stupid. In my head it seemed like such a good idea for us to wait until the time was right, but trying to verbalise that seemed pointless. "I don't know...it's just...well – I really like this guy. Every time we're together, I kind of get nervous and avoid anything happening. I want it to be just...right, you know? I've had so many disappointments in my life, but he seems to be the real deal...I just want to do the best with it" I said glancing down at the table. The next thing I realised, Debs had left her seat and had come over to hug me.

"Oh Rich, we're only teasing. I think it's kind of sweet that you're waiting for a good moment – it's lovely" and with that, gave me a peck on the cheek.

The conversation then turned back to sex and boys and we all shared stories of our worst shags (for the hundredth time). The girls had finished off one of the bottles of Sauvignon Blanc, so I went into the kitchen to grab the second bottle for them. As I did, I decided to be extra healthy and have a health shake to ensure I wouldn't be tempted by the wine. As I came back out onto the balcony, I put my drink down on the table and poured the wine for them.

"Cheers guys" says Debs as she leans across with her huge glass. I grin as I cheers her with my vanilla-flavoured protein shake.

"Enjoying your cum shake?" cackled Jacqui as she reached over to chink her wine glass with Debs and me.

"Honestly you two" I started, getting on my proverbial soap-box "I think you would be better off losing the wine and getting fit like me"

"Rich – it's been a morning and half an afternoon" Debs laughed in my face. "Don't start talking to us like you're this experienced health fanatic! Anyway, I don't think it's going to last. This is your thing – you get really excited by something and then end up chucking it in a few days later because you haven't got the ability to keep at anything."

I furrowed my brow and opened my mouth to retort, but Jacqui continued Debs' thought. "Remember the time you decided to take up piano? You wanted to impress some guy you were seeing, some musician. You sought out a top of the range tutor, went to two lessons and came back saying that he tried to hit on you."

"He did!" I said indignantly, turning to Jacqui to defend myself. "I couldn't go back – he was disgusting. He kept telling me how beautiful my playing was; even though we all know I couldn't play a note!"

"It's called encouragement! Anyway, what about the horse riding?" Jacqui continued.

"And fencing" countered Debs.

"Water polo"

"Tennis"

"Judo"

"Majorettes!" they chimed together, both of them laughing hysterically as I sat there giving them evils.

"You're supposed to support me" I said, getting cranky.

"Oh don't start sulking" said Jacqui, wiping the tears out of her eyes. "It's not that we don't support you, it's just that it's hard getting excited for you when we know that you're probably going to pack it in within ten days."

"I bet you a bottle that he won't even last five" said Debs, grinning.

"You're on" and Jacqui and Debs clinked glasses once more.

11pm update:
Dinner: Homemade vegetarian curry (using low-fat cream and no oil) and one light beer
Exercise: None (but I'd done a lot today including running and Tony)
Mood: Good
Number of texts to/from Dylan today in total: 26.

As I climbed into bed, I thought about what Jacqui and Debs were saying to me this afternoon. Did I really have such a flighty and fickle personality? Perhaps it wasn't a bad thing if I did – it just meant that I didn't want things to get too stale. Maybe that was why I hadn't had a boyfriend in years. I supposed it wasn't a bad thing that I couldn't commit to anything, given the work I did. Maybe I should have told the girls that it was quite a respectable way to be nowadays – at least I wouldn't end up disappointed if I didn't hang around too long. As I was lying there, my mind wandered back to my brief relationships, not that there were many – they were really more prolonged dates. I tried to locate the longest one but was at a loss to get past two months.

Meanwhile, people around me tended to bump into their life-partners on the way pick up a rental DVD or some other unlikely place. Three years later they were married, had two children and lived in a small flat in Chelsea. While I was indulging in my past, my mind focused on my first real crush; a guy named Christian. He was eighteen, I was fifteen, and of course I fell madly in love with him. I was like that back then: three dates and it was time to pick out the His & His porcelain cat collection.

I had met Christian on platform three of Victoria Station; he was on his way to London to visit his grandmother. I hadn't noticed him until I was running past him on the way to catch my train on the adjacent platform. As I was running along, trying to juggle my hold-all, daypack and Liberty carry bag, I saw him standing there, checking through his wallet. He was dressed in baggy cargos and a fitted, white vest, just like every other gay guy around that time – a timeless ensemble. His head was shaved and his blond fuzz was just begging to be rubbed. Then he looked up at me as I was madly rushing past, looking like an idiot, leering at him while three bags flew around my head as I tried to make my connecting train. I flashed him a quick smile and as I turned around I ran smack into a coffee stand. True to London style, everyone stopped momentarily, and then carried on with their business, walking around me, apart from one kind, old lady who stepped over me as I was grabbing for my bags. Like a moment where two lovers meet in a romance novel, he came over and helped me up, picking up my bags from the ground also. However, unlike the novels, the lead character had a welt on his head the size of Watford and was also bleeding from his top lip. The next few months were a whirlwind of sex, arguments and drinking. I supposed it was my own fault for getting too involved with him too quickly. He was just a regular lad who liked to hang out and wasn't interested in giving any devotion to anyone. I was absolutely devastated when he broke up with me. I remembered talking to a good friend at the time, who proffered the advice that, it usually took half as long as the length of a relationship to get over it. She was wrong - it took me just over two years.

11:15pm update:
Mood: Depressed (but quickly lifted by final unprompted good night text from Dylan)

The New Rich – Day 3 – On my back and legs over my head.

Really – Pilates looked so much easier when Madonna did it. I mean how hard was it to fold your legs behind your head? Thankfully I had dragged Jacqui along with me to the gym. Debs didn't want to have a bar of it, describing the idea as a waste of time since Pilates was "a pointless new phase that will go out, just like Step Aerobics". Jacqui seemed to be coping okay with the routine as she was a touch more bendy than I was, but had a bigger bottom. As she was breathing out, she delicately stretched and tipped her straightened legs over her head, touching her toes to the floor. My legs were akimbo and far from controlled and I was having trouble breathing since my body weight was bearing down on my bent neck and windpipe.

Jacqui had called me at my own bluff. Since she and the other wicked witch thought I had no will power or stamina, they decided to enrol me in a Pilate's class. When they first told me about it, my initial response was that I knew nothing about aircraft. Debs explained further and I scoffed at their plan.

"Ha, well, the only people that are gonna be shown a lesson is you two, my dears. Oh yes, *that* Pilates, I remember now. Well, I've not actually *done it* before." Suddenly gripped by a vague memory of my past, I conclude my water-tight argument. "In fact, my Gran used to be a contortionist." I assured them that since elasticity obviously ran in the family genes, I would have no problems. Speaking of elasticity, the instructor looked like some sort of double-jointed sadist who was probably able to tie himself in a bow and fit nicely into his own briefcase for easy travel. The positions he was showing us were quite amazing and although he was quite plain, I found myself getting strangely aroused. Adjusting my leotard, I pulled out of some sort of flower position and sat hunched on the mat, looking around the room. Boy did I feel stupid: my gym shorts had been in the wash after an accident with a beetroot and my new vegetable juicer and the only other pair of shorts I owned were bought in the early nineties. The latter of these shorts were the colour-changing type, responding to your body's heat. There was no way I was going to display my sweaty arse crack for anyone else to see.

Jacqui said she had something I could borrow and not to worry. Stupidly, I presumed it would have been a bog-standard pair of shorts. When she arrived at the gym and shooed me into the men's locker room with a plastic bag, I only then discovered my temporary attire. I didn't realise it was humanly possible to fit into a Lycra marble bag. The black, one-piece number was not only highlighting every dent and dimple on my body, I looked like I'd stepped out of an interpretive dance troupe.

Looking around the room now, in my tired state, I realised the error of my earlier comment. Gran wasn't a contortionist; actually the word I needed was exhibitionist. Cross-legged and panting, I recalled the time she was hauled up before the magistrate for the umpteenth time, while I sat there as a child, watching her protest her right to be at one with the world and be naked. Funnily enough, the magistrate agreed but threw in that she could be at one with the world and naked behind closed doors – however, he didn't think it entirely appropriate at the Bingo club.

The instructor barked another order and everyone in the room gracefully slinked into another position. I kept my head low and pretended to participate. The stitch in my stomach was paining me but I couldn't show Jacqui. She caught my eye and smiled while I smiled back and mouthed her a breathy hello. She hadn't even broken out into a sweat – and there I was red faced and puffing away like an old man of ninety.

"Right keep FITTERS! Warm up is OVER!" Up on your feet and we will BEGIN!" shouted the smug fucker at the front of the room.

I didn't know why he had to shout the last word of every sentence but I hated that instructor and wanted to pull his legwarmers up and garrotte him with them, but all I was able to do was groan as the workout began.

Two hours and fifteen minutes later we were back in the car.

"And how was it?" Debs asked, knowing full well how it would have gone. I pushed into the back seat, moving all the shopping that she had accumulated in our absence. I was still too out of breath to speak properly and only succeeded in giving a children's TV presenter-style thumbs up. Thankfully the conversation was left there. I let them think what they wanted anyway – I'd completed the stupid class and showed them that I could do it. After a long silence Jacqui mentioned that I only had another eleven to do and then the course would be over. *Yeah, along with my ability to walk* I thought as we drove home.

Later that afternoon, I had a nice chat to Dylan, and we made plans to meet for dinner and some drinks in Soho. The girls' hadn't popped in after my awful Pilates experience; they just scurried off home to change for their night out on the tiles. No doubt I would be getting a drunken call in the wee hours, unless I get to them first. I arranged to meet him around eight and already the butterflies in my tummy were fluttering.

It was almost eight o'clock and it was freezing – stupidly I'd chosen looks over warmth and decided not to wear a jacket – the wind was cutting right through my Ted Baker shirt. Dylan, thankfully, was right on schedule and looked perfect. He scooped me up in an embrace and we kissed before moving off to the restaurant. There was something really hot about kissing him in public – like a big middle finger to the rest of the world that had been scorning me for being single for so bloody long. His mouth tasted sexier than ever and I could quite easily have pulled him to the pavement and done him then and there, right by the ATM. As we walked, he told me all about his day; mundane things really but I was enthralled to be with him and hung on his every word. Our table was booked for a quarter to nine so we decided to go for a pre-dinner drink in a nearby bar. The evening was going well; we chatted and laughed, I was on top form and Dylan was lapping up my jokes and stories – it was probably the best date we'd had – that great mix of being with someone long enough to feel confident and comfortable, but still early enough in the relationship to have maximum excitement. We finished our drinks and as I got my wallet out, he told me that tonight was all on him. I stood outside by one of the street lights and waited for him to emerge from the bar, and when he did, wrapped his strong arms around my waist, planting a long kiss on my mouth.

"Mmm, what was that for?" I said when we eventually broke our kiss.

"Do I need a reason to kiss my boyfriend?" he grinned back at me. For a moment, I stopped and realised the importance of him calling me his boyfriend. I let out a sigh and before I realised what I was saying, I blurted out "I love y…"

Luckily I didn't finish my words, and he hadn't heard them properly as we were rudely interrupted.

"Dylan? Hey Dylan, How's it going?" We both swung around to see a handsome looking guy who came bounding over to hug Dylan. "I thought it was you!!" His blonde hair was jumping off his head in short, funky spikes and I noticed he was sexily un-shaven, reminding me a little of Justin Timberlake.

"Mark — er, hi. How are you?" As he spoke, he tried pathetically to pretend that they didn't know each other, but I knew full well they did.

"Yeah, good thanks, you're looking swell and still as handsome as ever" Mark took a step back, admiring Dylan in an appreciating manner. Who on earth used the word 'swell' as a compliment any more? More to the point, who used it even as an adjective? Dylan cut in, probably hoping to shut him up in case he was about to say anything else.

"This is my boyfriend; Rich. Actually, we're just off now, so catch up with you later, ok?" He was all flustered and I could tell he really didn't want to talk, or if he did, it was a conversation that certainly wasn't meant for my ears.

"Yeah, swell. Hey, I still got your number — was thinking I should call you up sometime soon — been a while since we…"

"Ok great! Nice catching up — bye!" Dylan cut him off with a touch too much enthusiasm, took my hand and literally pulled me along behind him. We walked in near silence, only breaking the quietness with pointless comments about things that really needn't be commented on.

I was doubly torn inside: did he hear me say I loved him, and who was Mark? I was aching to ask him but I couldn't get the words out. I tried to drop simple hints, but he was playing dumb.

"He seemed like a nice chap. Seemed…swell."

Dylan smiled awkwardly and kept quiet.

"He looked familiar, can't think where I've seen him before?" Still no response.

We continued to walk quietly until I couldn't help but blurt out. "Who was he?" catching my breath as I did so. We stopped in the middle of the street causing the people marching behind us to tut loudly and go around us. Facing each other, I asked again but in a much softer voice.

"Who was he? It's ok – you can talk to me about past boyfriends, it's ok." He looked at me but I could see he didn't want to talk about it.

"He is…, I mean, he *was* a client of mine. He's never been a boyfriend and I don't have any emotional feelings for him. It was just sex, you know how it goes." I couldn't get any words out, forcing him to repeat himself. "It's just sex right? We might even see some of your clients around town tonight; it's not a big deal" he shrugged, but it was for me. All my paranoia's started to beat me up; my insecurity, my fear, my unnecessary worry; all of them took a good, hard slug.

I had to give him the benefit of the doubt, what else could I have done but bury my concerns as best I could. For the next ten minutes we walked again in silence, finally reaching the restaurant and picking up where we had left off. As we ate, we got lost in conversation and Mark had been forgotten. The food was amazing; I had never tasted so many wonderful things. The champagne was delightful and after a couple of glasses I felt myself easing up. Then, like something out of a cheesy film, he cut some of his food and spoon fed me. Had I been watching such a display being done in a restaurant by some loved up couple, I probably would have thrown a bread roll at them, but as it was, to have such a small, cute gesture made to you in person was quite touching.

After the main course, we decided to get one dessert and share. The other diners were finishing off their coffees and settling the cheques while Dylan and I made eyes to each other over our sticky toffee pudding. I was just about to spoon another mouthful to him when his phone beeped. I looked at him, he looked at me. I wanted to ask who it was, knowing it was none of my business, but still hoping he would have divulged. He didn't and after reading it just tucked it back into his pocket. Now my mind had another reason to tick. I forced myself to stay quiet, shovelling a big spoonful of pudding into my mouth. Then I tried to pick up the conversation where we left off, but his phone beeped again. I set my spoon down into the bowl sharply and looked over to him. He read the message, typed a reply and set the phone down on the table. He must have seen I looked annoyed and assured me it was no one. When his phone beeped for a third time I instantly flew to take it but he beat me to it and at the same time sent a glass of champagne sailing off the table and landing in his lap. I wanted to laugh but lucky I didn't; he was cursing under his breath.

When he excused himself to go clean up, I thought I was being a very good boyfriend and took his phone to dry it off. As I wiped at gently, I went into the menu and a cold chill struck me. Seeing the name 'Mark' left a nasty swirling in my tummy - this time they weren't butterflies, but huge, ugly moths. He returned, still dabbing at his jeans and immediately saw his phone that I had put back next to his plate, where he had left it. Neither of us said a word.

The rest of the evening wasn't as good when it had started; I still had a lingering, sour mood peppered with unwanted thoughts of Mark. I forced myself to understand that I was just being paranoid and not to let it ruin the rare quality time that we had together.

As the evening drew to a close, my hunger for Dylan had been sated by seeing him tonight and we walked to the tube station hand in hand along a street that was still bustled with excited clubbers. Outside Leicester Square station, we locked in another kiss, much to the disgust of some posh theatre-goers nearby. I didn't care, I felt totally rested when I was in his arms.

"So, give you a call during the week?" he still held my hand as he spoke and immediately pulled me back for another kiss. My thoughts flashed back to that chat I'd had with Jacqui and Debs on my balcony; why was I so nervous about being with him sexually? If I kept waiting for the perfect opportunity, maybe it would never come and I'd end up shooting myself in the foot.

"Yeah, good idea. Or...?"

"Or?" smiled Dylan.

"Or if you like...you could...come back to mine?"

A smile stretched across his face. "I thought you'd never fucking ask, where's the bus stop?"

Back at the flat, I fumbled with the key noisily in the lock. I hadn't drunk much, but Dylan kissing me gently on the back of my neck gave me the same heady feeling of being drunk and uncaring. We fell into the hall and began ripping at each other's clothes, trying to kick our shoes off and almost falling on top of each other in the dark – it was as if tonight's ugliness hadn't even happened. He pinned me against the wall and kissed me intensely, passionately, hungrily. I fumbled with his belt and then with his fly, and as his jeans dropped to his ankles, I grabbed his arse like it was going out of fashion.

"You're amazing" he growled in a breathy whisper, then picked me up and carried me to the bedroom, after carrying me to the bathroom first by mistake.

In bed he was tender and considerate, but still lusty and forceful. His hands over my body felt like they had been there forever and seemed to know every inch of flesh that I needed him to touch. We rolled around on the bed, getting tangled in the sheets and in each other, and just at the right moments he would hold me tightly and look deeply into my eyes before kissing me. By ten past three, I had fallen into a deep sleep while I lay across his chest, holding his hand lightly. I woke early to feel him still holding me in a spoon; it was the perfect way to start a lazy Sunday together. I wanted to roll over and kiss him while he slept, but didn't want to disturb him so I nestled back into his warm body and let myself drift off again. The next time I woke was a little after eleven when his phone beeped yet again. He leapt out of bed still half asleep and blearily read his message.

"Shit. I'm gonna have to make a move babe. I have to work today."

I knew it was Mark but I didn't say anything. Disappointed, I pulled the duvet up over my head and sulked quietly while he dressed in silence. Before he left, he kissed me on the cheek and said he would call me later, and as the door closed behind him I sat up angrily, not really knowing what to do. I was angry and jealous and wanted to call him to tell him not to bother calling me, that this obviously was a mistake and that he should just leave me alone, but I knew I didn't mean any of that at all. I just wished that after such an amazing night together, we could have followed it with some time together.

I sighed and lay back down. I wanted him back with me, but had to make do with the smell of his fading aftershave on the pillow beside me as I fell asleep on his side of the bed.

Juan was supposed to have met me over half an hour ago, but then again why did I never learn; he always arrived late for everything. I meandered around in the ticket hall looking increasingly shifty as I waited. Hunger ripped at my stomach as I hadn't bothered with breakfast – after all, we had planned to meet nice and early for a run around Hyde Park. I decided to call Dylan to kill some time and to make myself feel less exposed; I was dressed in a tracksuit, something I never normally wore. There was no reply so I huddled back in the corner and carried on waiting for Juan. When I had asked him to come with me I fully expected him to laugh and hang up, but he actually agreed. I thought he was showing that he could be a wonderful and devoted friend by lending me support, but actually he blabbed that he thought he had cellulite and was really only in it for what he could get out of it.

I checked my watch again; 9:12am, and then I heard him call out to me from the top of the escalator.

"Coo-ee sweetie, god, your always bloody early!" typical Juan, turning it around again – it probably didn't even cross his mind we were supposed to meet at half past eight. "Guess who wanted some arse before he went home" he continued "the guy who drove a Bentley! I hope I can still run?" His voice echoed around the ticket hall as he sashayed down the escalator, morning commuters looking positively disturbed. To be honest, in his world there was no room for subtle; he didn't care who heard what he got up to, dismissing them only as jealous or envious and as he bounded to the bottom of the escalator I noticed that his attire was also less than subtle.

"What have you come as? We are going for a run."

"I know we are sweetie, I'm all ready, see?" he took a step back to ensure he was in total public view and peeled off his leather jacket to reveal a lurid all-in-one silver tracksuit. On his feet was a pair of the biggest trainers I had ever seen, and when he turned to show off his ensemble, I couldn't help but notice that from the side view he looked like a golf club. His outfit was of course complemented by a pair of ridiculously gigantic sunglasses.

"You like? McQueen!" He said with glee.

He waved the jacket at me to get me to hold it and I complied with a sigh while he minced out of the station much to the amusement of the gathering crowd around him.

"And just what do you expect me to do with this" I shouted after him, waving it around.

"Put it in your bag darling."

I gritted my teeth. "I don't have a bag, I told you we were going running. Why didn't you bring one if you insisted on wearing it?" He stopped and turned to me, lifting the visor off his face.

"With *this* outfit?" his mouth hung momentarily in a pout before he replaced his goggles and jogged out onto the zebra crossing outside the station. I moped behind with his jacket bundled up into a ball. Almost immediately, motorists were slowing down from all sides, their occupants leering from windows to take in the sight. I sighed and tried to catch up with him as he powered ahead over the crossing and into the park. I wondered if people were thinking that one of the street artists from Covent Garden had gotten tired of standing stock still and had decided to have a little wander.

The sun was unsympathetic as we walked into the park. I called to Juan who was now fast-walking to the centre with much gusto.

"This looks like a good spot – we could do a lap here and see how we feel after?" I said, realising he couldn't even hear me. "Oh is it Rich?" I replied to myself mockingly. "Yes Rich, it is".

He stopped and faced me with a quizzical expression. Perhaps he did hear after all? "What about my jacket?" Good question, what about his jacket. Neither of us had a bag and it was really heating up. "We can put it in the coat check?" he said looking around for the facilities.

"Coat che….it's a public park!" I spat. He tutted loudly and rested his hands on his hips.

"Well, I can't carry it, I'll crease. Do you really want that on your conscience today?" I had to bite my tongue.

"Well, the only thing we can do…" I said, pointing to a landscaped flowerbed.

"You're not serious!" he squealed, following my finger.

"Why not, no one is around. It's a quiet corner, trust me, it'll be fine" He stood there, lifted his sunglasses and eyeballed me as if this was going to turn into some showdown from the Wild West. "Fine then" I said, going for a change in tack "just let me know when you get too hot from carrying it, come to think of it I'll probably notice when you collapse into a hyperventilating heap on the ground" I said trying to alarm him. It didn't work but I carried on. "and when you're sweating, your foundation has run you're on the ground, muddy and tired and generally looking worse for wear....." That worked and immediately he agreed. I made sure no one was around and then squeezed myself between the wall and the line of bushes, crouching down and tucking his jacket far under a shrub.

"Will you stop worrying? We'll do a lap or two and then come back to get it. You're such a worrier. I know exactly where we are."

At long last we both managed start our run and did a solid fifteen minutes before slowing to a stop. Falling onto a nearby bench we both deserved a rest.

"I can't believe you're running with me." I said with a big grin on my face "I'm very impressed – you've shown a side of you that I hadn't seen before, well done. Mind you – glad we stopped, my chest is aching – you too?"

"No sweetie, I could run for hours if I had to. I shouldn't have put a thong on today – it's riding up me something chronic."

"Well, thong or not, you're not bailing on me now – come on, lets complete a lap at least, then we'll have a brisk walk? Come on, before it gets any hotter."

As we started off again he pulled down the zip on his track top to his navel, revealing a bronzed, bare chest. "What? It's hot! Don't want me over-heating do you?" I shook my head and carried on running. Five minutes later, on another park bench, we sat, this time not speaking, but gasping for tiny breaths of air. This health kick of mine was going to take years before I got into shape.

The tinkling of an ice cream van sounded in our ears before it set up camp a few feet away and children had already clambered over each other to get there first. Juan looked at me without turning his head completely and I did the same to him. He snapped his eyes straight ahead, towards the van.

"Oh Rich, it's so hot! I'm so worn out!" I knew what he was about to suggest but I let him carry on over-acting. He looked at me, looked at the ice cream van, looked at me again and then let out the heaviest sigh. "And my throat – it's so dry! Plus we *have* been running for *ages*!" I looked as far left as I could and could still see the entrance to the park where we started, barely a couple of hundred feet away.

Several minutes later I plonked myself back on the bench and handed him his double scoop with extra flake while I slurped on my Cola lolly.

"I hope you eat better when you're at work!" he laughed. I didn't reply.

We carried on eating our cooling treats as the ice cream van moved off to another packed area. After we finished, we got up, fully intending to jog, but somehow we ended up on a lovely patch of grass by the boating pond, stretched out and catching some rays. Juan had taken his top off and was lying face down; I had only dared to roll the sleeves up on my t-shirt.

"How did this happen? Weren't we supposed to be jogging?"

"We *did* jog, now we rest. We don't want to overdo it on the first day."

We spent the rest of the morning boy-watching and talking about sex. In the early afternoon he nipped over the road and came back with a bottle of Chardonnay and some polystyrene cups. We polished it off before it warmed through too much, and relaxed, thinking that exercise didn't have to be all hard work. All too soon the sun slid behind some dark clouds and the wind picked up a little, so we decided to call it a day and head off when suddenly he let out a shriek and dropped the empty wine bottle on the grass. "My jacket, quick, where's my jacket?"

Forty five minutes later we sat at a booth in a bar, just by the park, and I poured a hearty glass of red to console him. After trudging back to where we started, the jacket was nowhere to be seen. I looked down at my mud-stained hands and nails; of course it had been me who had to scrabble around in the dirt looking for it. I had done my best to try and cheer him up, telling him that it really wasn't anyone else's fault but his own and that if hadn't brought it along in the first instance then I wouldn't have had to bury his seven hundred pound jacket in a shallow grave. Needless to say, it did little to soothe him. In fact, as I was drinking and he was sulking, I noticed the Big Issue vendor standing outside on the street. He was typical looking really, long hair, shuffling from foot to foot, jeering politely at passers by, tucking his cold hands into the pockets of his leather jacket…leather jacket! I nudged Juan and gestured for him to look and identify if it could have been his.

"The thieving gypsy!" he squeaked, confirming that it was indeed his. At that point I quietly reminded him that it probably wasn't good form to attempt a crash tackle on homeless person and rip his jacket off his back, even if it was stolen. Sighing heavily he chugged back wine. He had never really attached himself to anyone, and the fact that he once tried to divorce both his parents at the age of fifteen only attested to this. He loved his clothes though, there was no denying that. Every Prada, Gucci and Dior was lovingly filed away in his walk-in room ("closet is so limiting, pet", he would often say to me). Walking into that converted spare room was the gay man's equivalent of a child being let loose in Disneyland. There were sliding draws of ties, moving racks of suits, glass-covered display cases of cufflinks, tie clips and miscellaneous jewellery.

As he impatiently fingered a coaster, he told me about the many times he lovingly wore that jacket out. Usually though, it ended up on the floor with him kneeling on it so he wouldn't graze his knees when blowing someone. Suddenly, I had the most daring idea - I decided it was my time to act in his best interest and drained the rest of my merlot.

"Meet me out the front in ten minutes". Before he could say anything, I was striding out of the bar like a man on a mission. As I stepped outside and caught a glance of myself in the reflection of the window, I ruffled up my hair and took off my t-shirt, exposing my tight running vest, pulled up my running shorts a little higher to show off more thigh and finally adjusted my crotch, making it look as full as I could. While my hands were down my pants I happened to look past my reflection, into the bar. There, sitting at the booth by the window and staring at me in horror was my old boss, his wife and their teenage son; all of them frozen in mid-motion, their beer-battered chips halfway to their mouths.

"Oh...hello" I waved cheerily through the window at the three of them. Good to see I was giving the impression that I had landed on my feet after leaving my last real employment.

I tucked my t-shirt into the back of my pants, puffed up my chest and walked to the Big Issue vendor.

"Hi there..." I glanced down to his official lanyard, half expecting it to say "I'm homeless, ask me how". "How are you today, Robert?" I soldiered on, noting the look on his face as he stared contemptuously at me.

"Big Issue?" he droned back at me, obviously having sold it for so long he had forgotten how to interact with random and admittedly cute strangers.

"No thanks...I was hoping I could interest *you* in something actually" I said moving forward and smiling somewhat, doing my best bar-moves on him. He just looked me up and down, not fully understanding what I was hinting at. "I have a thing for...rough guys" I purred, stepping even closer, ignoring the stench of him.

"What the fuck is wrong with you?" he said putting his magazines on a small table next to him.

"I..." I stammered trying to think of what to say next...oh fuck it; I just had to take a leaf out of Juan's book. "Look, I'll make it easy for you – if you come with me right now into the toilets in that bar over there, I'll give you the best blowjob of your life. A mouth is a mouth, and right now I'm hungry for what you're packing down there."

He man squinted hard at me, looking like he was about to beat the shit out of me.

"You can stand there getting all defensive, or you can blow a load and be back in the street in ten minutes...up to you." I put the best disinterested look I could muster on my face and looked him directly in the eye. He didn't say anything but returned my stare with defiance. It was like an old showdown from the Midwest – minus the horses, saloon and spurs. Okay, so it was nothing like a showdown. Suddenly he adjusted his crotch with his hand. Bingo.

"I gotta be quick" he said looking around furtively.

"There are some toilets in that bar, plenty of room in the stalls" I grinned knowing exactly how to play the next part of this. As I walked back into the bar with him in tow, I casually glanced across to Juan who was sitting and staring at me, mouth agape. I met his eye and pulled one of my hands up to my chest making a quick "drink up" signal to him. Thankfully the bathrooms were deserted when I pushed open the door. I crossed the tiled floor to the last stall and as the door was half closing behind me, it opened again and in came the seller behind me. I looked casually back over my shoulder and then went into the cubicle. To say there was no room was an understatement; he was pretty much on top of me as soon as we got in. I closed the door and turned to him, reluctant to actually rub his crotch but knowing that I only had minutes to get this over with. I held my breath and placed my left hand on his packet while starting to remove his jacket with my right.

"What are you doing" he said, trying to pull it back on.

"God, relax, I'm just going to put it under my knees." He shrugged it off and it dropped to the floor. Next I undid his jeans, noticing the grubby marks around the fly. They too dropped to the floor. He was wearing grey briefs: unfortunately I think they used to be white. I pulled them down too. Looking at the shrivelled piece that was lying there looking up at me, I didn't t know how women put up with some guys. Surrounding it was a forest of pubes and pimples. I wanted to vomit but started to work him over with my hands, knowing full well there was no way I was putting my mouth around it; who knew where had been. He closed his eyes and leant back. That was my chance! I flicked the jacket from under my knees to outside the stall. Acting on impulse and not really knowing what to do next I spat on my hand to get him wet and I whispered "you know I would so love for you to shove that up me. Oh baby, yeah I want you so bad, my arse is so tight and aching for you" I pulled out my best smut talk as he opened his eyes and looks down at me.

"You got a rubber on you?" he asked obviously not caring what or who he stuck his dick into. A perfect specimen of a man; get him horny and he'd let you do whatever you wanted.

"Hang on, there's a machine next to the hand dryer" I said getting off my knees and turning around. I opened the door to the cubicle and glanced out, thankfully the coat was off to the side and he couldn't see it from where he was sitting. All I had to do was close him in the cubicle and then it would be freedom.

"Wait" he said. I turned around and looked at him as he was playing with himself, "get the extra large!" I smiled knowing full well he'd have been hard pressed to adequately fill a shot glass.

I ran out of the bathroom with the coat in one hand like a madman. Juan was standing near the door of the bar and we both burst into the street in gales of laughter. We didn't stop running until we're three blocks away – ironically it was more exercise than we had done all day. He turned to me, puffing away madly.

"Sweetie, you are the best fucking whore I know!" Coming from him that was the nicest thing he could have said.

London Independent Hospital, A&E department.

Number 202 flashed up on the display, signalling for a sad, looking man with a heavily, bleeding hand to make his way to the examination room. I checked my number for the umpteenth time; 223, and sighed, shifting in my hard, plastic chair, trying to get comfortable. The woman sitting next to me huffed under her breath every time I did so I turned to her and huffed back louder.

That morning, Dylan had woken me with a call to say hi and that he was missing me, and I had been treating myself to a lay-in because every muscle in my body ached from all the exercise and running I had been doing. We chatted for a while; it felt so good to hear his voice. After an hour or so of small talk I hung up, deciding on a late breakfast - if it was ok to call it breakfast at 1pm. The longer we had been seeing each other, the more awkward I was feeling about shagging other guys, even though it was my job, and I wondered if he felt the same as I did. It was probably far too soon to dare bring it up in conversation.

I had a job booked for four o clock; Adam and his boyfriend wanted me for a threesome party; apparently I had been suggested to them by one of my other clients who happened to know them. Anyway, I arranged to meet them – the only issue was where we were to do this as Adam lived with his parents and his boyfriend, Ryan, was lodging with a nice family in Reading. As nice as they were though, I doubt they would have turned a blind eye to the spit roasting taking place whilst they enjoyed their dinner and the X Factor. I had never allowed clients to come to my flat, but I had agreed when they said they would pay extra. I had probably just stepped over the line of professional standards for my profession, if my profession even *had any.*

They arrived a little later than arranged, but when they finally did I wasn't upset. The handsome couple strode into my apartment with a sexy air of manly arrogance – I felt myself get a little weak-kneed. Both of them were towering over six feet and judging by their physiques, they could have easily just stepped out of military training school.

I welcomed them in and they sat on my sofa while we had a little polite chat, some drinks and I reiterated my charges. Truth be told, I would have happily let them bang me without any mention of money – they were gorgeous. Adam got out a bulging wallet and slapped it on the coffee table; that wasn't the only thing about Adam that bulged though. I was about to lead them to my bedroom when they decided to strip then and there, and I felt it would be terribly rude of me to interrupt them.

At first they kissed each other passionately while their wandering hands entertained each other's bodies; I looked on jealously as their toned bodies seemed to ripple in all the right places. I couldn't hold back any longer and literally dived between them for a piece of the action, screaming silent thanks in my head. Next they were kissing me, kissing each other, then a three-way kiss; I was surely about to explode. The feel of their big hands over my body was electrifying.

As I was about to move on to second base, I saw Ryan had already beaten me to it and was kneeling before Adam. Was it normal for me to wait my turn? I'd only ever been in one-on-one action before. Adam moaned while Ryan blew him, and seeing that I was left out, with no effort at all he pulled me toward him with a strong arm and kissed me hard with his hand on the back of my head. After that he began pushing me down to where Ryan was – ok, I got the idea and decided to play along, resisting the urge to kick Ryan out of the way totally. Mother had always told me share and share alike. How true her words seemed now.

As things progressed, it was time to get a bit heavier and we all found ourselves on the floor. Ryan growled what he wanted to do to me and frankly, I had no problem with it. Adam joined in and told me of his plans too. As I was bending over it suddenly went quiet behind me so I presumed that they were both rubbering up. When I turned round to check, I couldn't have been more wrong as they were both kneeling behind me, jostling each other. Adam was staring at Ryan and suddenly exploded.

"I'm fucking him first, we discussed this on the phone, remember?"

"So? I *said* it first to him first, so therefore I am."

"No. If I don't go first, then it's not happening. Me first, right Rich?"

I was a little stunned and blurted out that I really didn't mind.

"You *always* do this; you *always* ruin it, don't you" bleated Adam.

"Why are you getting so upset? He obviously wants me first, deal with it." Ryan knelt behind me and took hold of my waist. Adam shoved Ryan's hands out of the way; he took hold of my waist next. Then Ryan pushed Adam out of the way and grabbed me. Then Adam. Then Ryan. They were actually fighting over me. This wasn't going well so I wriggled free of their hold and sat watching their display with disbelief.

"You fucking cow, I am doing him first! You have to wait – you can't always have it your way."

"Don't you call me a fucking cow, you bitch"

"What are you gonna do about it...COW"

"You little...." Then the two boys began wrestling each other to the ground and I would have said the punches flew, but they were more slaps really.

"OW, that really HURT you frigid cow. Get off me!"

"Frigid? Why you 'roided-up skank, at least I'm not thinning on top!

As I sat staring in horror and hilarity, I lost track of who was screaming what insult to whom, but one of them screamed like a girl.

"Get OFF my hair – you little.....frigid....BITCH!"

"I am NOT frigid – Rich, I am NOT frigid!"

"You are!"

I pulled on my track bottoms and hurried to the kitchen, unsure how to deal with this. I poured myself a Tropicana – took a sip, then added a hefty measure of gin. I drank it down in one gulp, and poured a further shot of gin.

As I heard the screaming and cat-calling from the next room, I had to shake my head in disbelief. Was this really happening to me? In my living room were two of the sexiest lads I had seen outside of the Abercrombie & Fitch website, and they were rolling around on my rug firing catty insults and bitch slapping each other – surely not? I had the intention of storming in and breaking it up, but when I stood in the doorway looking at them, it seemed best not to intervene. Adam had Ryan in a move that seemed to mirror a gymnast's best performance; meanwhile, Ryan had his legs clenched around Adam's head. At first glance it was very sexy and looked like they were shagging, but then Adam reached Ryan's nipple and gave it a hard tweak, causing Ryan to drop him instantly.

"Er, boys…should we, er, boys?" I half-shouted.

The pair continued to roll about and the name calling was getting breathy and vicious.

"Silly…little…bitch….AND you're putting on weight!"

"Can….you blame…me…when my…FRIGID cow of a boyfriend goes out all night…and I…sit home having a more intense relationship…with the…FRIDGE?!"

I decided not to break it up – they were like two dogs fighting over a bone, quite literally.

Just then the remote control flew past my head.

"Hey!" I shouted. When my furniture became involved I decided so would I. "Will you just get out of my flat!" I barked angrily, but remembering the sheer size of them both I added a considerate 'Please'.

The remote control was followed by a DVD of *Uncle Buck*. *Uncle Buck* was followed by *The Best of Sheena Easton* (a present I hasten to add). When my *Five Star* three-disc box set got fingered, enough was enough. I threw myself onto the fighting pair and tried to wrench them apart. If I heard the words cow, bitch or frigid once more, I was going to inflict pain on them both – this, I discovered from my viewing so far could've been achieved by calling one of them fat and the other bald.

They finally separated, gasping for breath and covered in sweat. I still wanted them to do me, but thought it slightly inappropriate to mention this now. As I drew breath to say something sensible about a cup of herbal tea and a chat about what had just happened, they locked together once again in a barrage of insults and hair pulling.

"ENOUGH!" I screamed, but as I got to my feet I was brought crashing down to the floor by a sudden and loud crack to my shin. Ryan had swiped at Adam with a dumb-bell which had been sitting near the couch because Adam had called him a mincing Mary with breasts. Having missed Adam, he caught me on my lower leg and my world went white and left me seeing stars. Pain surged through my body with lightning speed; I felt like someone had started a fire inside my leg it was that intense. As I cried out in pain, the squabbling quietened down and both the boys realised it was time to stop. They dressed hurriedly and said they were taking me to the hospital. I couldn't even respond as I was doubled up in pain. As I lay in the back of their car, I was shaken about as they screeched their way to A&E. They even had the nerve to carry on their verbal abuse while I was sobbing in the back seat.

They tore away from the hospital, leaving me to hobble into the disinfectant-smelling building, and I was given a number from the miserable nurse behind the desk, and then found a seat to collapse in. Two and a half painful hours later, I was dismissed from Dr Finnegan's office with the diagnosis. My shin had been badly bruised, but luckily it wasn't broken. When she had asked me how I came by this injury, I told her that exercise was dangerous and that fat people had the right idea. I neglected to include the part about *Brokeback Mountain* meets *WWF*.

As I left the cab outside my front door, I paid the cab driver thirty-two pounds plus tip; I waddled into my living room and sat in silence, wanting to cry. I also wanted to eat the tub of ice cream in my freezer, but it hurt too much to move. I even thought about texting someone to come over and fetch it for me.

Maybe it was the pain killers I was prescribed but I soon dozed off and had a lovely dream about a giant tub of Ben & Jerry's that was fighting an Android. The Android was calling the ice cream fat and taunting it for having love handles. The ice cream then said it was allergic to exercise but the only type it would undertake in was sex, but only with the Android. They actually did get it on but the ice cream started to melt causing the Android to short circuit. I woke with a start after a tingling sensation on my face - I had fallen asleep on my phone and it was half-embedded into my cheek. I peeled it away, gently rubbing my cheek and looking around to see where I was as I still felt disoriented.

Immediately my eyes rested on Adam's wallet on the coffee table. He must have left it there before they rushed me to the hospital. I reached for my mobile and sure enough there was a text from him asking if his wallet was there. I deleted it.

Two days later I was able to hobble around with a little more comfort, but the bruise that erupted on my leg was enormous. The important thing was that I hadn't done any lasting damage to my leg or my career. I had to get this wallet back to Adam somehow so called up Debs who came over with fruit and magazines. I told her all about everything and she thought the whole thing really funny – which made me laugh and see the comedic side of the whole event.

She was right though, who else did this happen to apart from me. After a few hours of her nursing around me, she said she would post the wallet back to him and we rummaged through it for an address. However, by the time the wallet would reach him, it would've been considerably lighter as I made sure I took my fee and some extra to cover the cab fare and the emotional damage they had inflicted on me.

After Debs left, I sat with tired thoughts, my mind turning to Dylan instinctively. I felt a flush of guilt and slight panic at the fact I had clients in my apartment. I dialled his number, aching to hear his voice, but feeling he knew what I had been up to. Of course, he had no way of knowing – and even if he did – he knew what I did for work, but it still felt wrong. I put my worry to the back of mind when I heard his voice and we chatted long into the night.

Tuesday afternoon, working in Woking.

His eyes looked up at me wilfully as he placed his hand on my groin again, this time tightening his grip.

"Ohh, yeah, you're a big boy, ooh baby" and he made a noise that sounded like a sharp inhale of breath after swallowing a mouth whistle. "How are we doing, anything?" he asked, stepping back out of his brief characterisation.

I shook my head. "Sorry, no. I don't know what's wrong with me; I never usually get this…problem."

I was lying; I knew full well what was wrong with me. I had been fine when I boarded the train from London Paddington and I was fine as I sat with my iPod on full blast. I was so fine that even when the ticket inspector came around, I wasn't consumed by my regulatory moment of panic that always seemed to engulf me even though I had paid the fare. It was also true to say I was fine as I got off the train and met Simon at lunchtime as planned. We dallied with pathetic small talk and English pleasantries as we drove to his place, and we very soon moved to the master bedroom where I was more than happy to whip it out, whip him over and give it to him hard. However, as my mind fluttered over Dylan for only a second or two my enthusiasm had quickly vanished, along with my erection. I rested back on my heels and sat looking at him. As he lay there looking up at me wearing nothing but a t-shirt, he reminded me of an overgrown baby; bald as a coot, face bright pink and round, and his eyebrows were so fine that they almost looked hairless. His legs were still up on my shoulders and I rested my hands on them casually.

"Um, anything else I can do for you instead?" I offered, sounding like a baker who has just run out of soy-linseed loafs.

"Nope" he said with a deflated voice. I looked down to where his t-shirt ended and his flabby pinkness begun, and seeing that he certainly hadn't lost *his* enthusiasm, I began to go down on him until I felt his hand on my head stopping me. "No, I don't like that" he protested. How can anyone not like it? It was the laziest way to orgasm, surely?

"Oh, you haven't had me do it yet – trust me, it's what I'm known for" I said as I pushed against his hand and went down again. Before I'd even made contact with it, he let out a shrill of giggles followed by an immediate apology. This was followed by another set of giggles and another apology. I was losing my momentum as his body kept jerking with laughter.

"I'm sorry, I'm sorry – I'm too ticklish down there and you'll have to stop. We'll have to do something else. This is the only night I've had off work for weeks, if I don't get a fat cock up me tonight and blow my load, then I'll probably die of cum poisoning and that's not a thought I relish. So come on, you're the expert – what can you do to me, if you can't....do *that*?"

I thought long and hard, cursing myself for not being long and hard, but I had to give this guy something. We could put some porn on, but that didn't really do anything for me unless I watched it alone - I found it quite sordid when somebody else was in the room. I could jerk him off, but he wouldn't pay the full amount, I could have let him do me, but that wasn't what he wanted, so, given the lack of choices, I reluctantly raised the suggestion of putting on a dirty movie. His face lit up and he pranced over to his chest of drawers, his cock still sticking out before him proudly. I had a very high sex drive and usually got hard at the change of the winds direction, but all those other times I hadn't been thinking about Dylan. Simon turned back to me and I had to try hard to take my eyes off his still-hard cock.

"What do you prefer" he asked as if he were working behind the counter at HMV. "We have *AssBusters* or *The Rugby Coach 2* – both as good as each other really, but rugby is a tad hotter."

"And if I haven't seen *The Rugby Coach 1*...?"

Simon responded by holding up the cover in his right hand. "Um...I don't think you need to see the first one. Let's watch this one to whet your appetite." Clearly he missed the subtle humour in life. He put the DVD on and settled back next to me on the bed, his cock was *still* hard and I was feeling a little intimidated. The screen came to life and the dodgy credits rolled by to reveal starring names like Randy Horn and Dick McMassive. The picture was a little too realistic, making it look like we were invading someone's life. It was set in an all-American High School, complete with jocks, banners, and sports equipment. We were in the sports hall and there was an exchange going on between what appeared to be student and teacher.

[Jimmy] "But coach, if you don't put me on the team, my mom will be pissed."
[Coach] "Jimmy – I just can't do it, you know that you're playing sucked out there today"
[Jimmy] "But coach, I gotta play!"

Coach was a big burly man, looking a very handsome forty something. His chest was over-inflated in a tight-fitting singlet and his shorts were more like hot pants they were that tight around his burly legs. Little Jimmy wasn't that little - in fact, he seemed to be the same age as the coach, but under all that make-up and blonde floppy hair, he was desperately trying to pass himself off as a sixteen year old jock. His jaw wasn't so much chiselled, but more angled, a bit like a cartoon superhero. Of course, both men were stunningly good looking – typical.

[Jimmy] "Coach, I, I…"
[Coach] "Jimmy – I don't know what else to say."
[Jimmy] "Maybe I can…"
[Coach] "What Jimmy?"
[Jimmy] "….do something to change your mind coach?"
[Coach] "What do you mean Jimmy?"
[Jimmy] "Maybe my playing isn't the only thing I suck at?

Within a few minutes, Jimmy had persuaded coach to step out of his clothing and was now giving him a blowjob in the middle of the sports hall. The two of them then proceeded to have sex at gravity-defying angles all over the place. I wasn't getting turned on at all; it was actually having a reverse affect on me. I could sense Simon trying to make a move but I didn't want him touching my deflated cock and making matters worse. After a while he was getting the idea that it wasn't working but didn't switch off the video. We had to resort to watching hard porn while engaging in polite conversation throughout.

"Have you lived here long then?"

"Few months, I like it."

[Coach] "I'm gonna plough your fucking ass boy, you like that?"

"Nice area. Very…quiet."

"[Jimmy] "Fuck yeah, teach me coach, pound me hard!"

"Yeah, yeah. It's nice."

[Coach] "Ohhh, that feels good!"

"Cool."

This went on until the coach and Jimmy were spent, and Simon hit the zapper making the screen go blank. He let out a sigh so loud that it made me uncomfortable. The film had been playing for about fifty minutes and he had kept his stiffy throughout. I decided then that he wasn't normal.

"I have an idea" Simon said as he leapt off the bed to get something out of the chest of drawers. He waddled back toward me with something hidden behind his back.

"Ta-da!"

He held out a veiny, pink dildo before me like some sort of crazed, dismembered offering.

"It's my dildo."

"I sure can see it's a dildo."

"I'll lube up – then you can fuck me, without fucking me, cool huh?"

I was a bit shocked but had decided halfway through the film that I really just wanted to get this gig over and done with, so I nodded my head in agreement. I approached him from behind while he was kneeling on the bed, arse stuck out high in the air. When I usually did a guy I didn't really need to look where I was putting it, I just knew what went where. But having it displayed before me, well, it was a test of will to say the least. As I made contact with him, his body quivered with anticipation. To Simon this was heaven on a plate – to me it was more like the leftovers that had gone a bit spongy. Thankfully after only a few minutes he exploded into orgasm, coating the sheets and some of the pillow that was underneath him.

"Wow, that was great" I said, wiping my brow, feigning enjoyment and exertion from the event. I jumped up and almost ran to the bathroom desperate for the sink.

"Oh Rich – that was fucking HOT!"

By this time I was furiously scrubbing my hands; I felt so dirty and no amount of scrubbing would erase this event from my mind.

"Rich –?" he called out again.

Yeah, whatever...dirty fuckwit I mumbled to myself. I smiled as I walked back into the bedroom, still acting like I'd enjoyed myself...that was until the money was handed over.

"So – we'll do this again, yeah?" he asked as he threw the towel onto the bed and reached for his wallet. I was pulling up my jeans when my phone rang. I knew from the ring tone that it was Dylan. I didn't answer it, but took the money without speaking. As I headed for the door, I turned to Simon, Dylan still heavy on my mind.

"You know what?" I said looking him square in the face, "I think it's best if you just delete my number. I'm thinking I might try and do something else for a while. Sorry, but I'm sure there are plenty more...er, you know."

He looked for a moment before resting his hand on my shoulder. I thought he was going to say something nice and understanding; congratulating me for trying to better myself – instead he just pushed me out the door and closed it in my face.

Out in the darkening street, the fresh air against my skin felt cool and refreshing, although it didn't quell the fire that still burned in my stomach when I thought about Dylan. I felt so guilty and ashamed and embarrassed, but why? He knew what I was doing for money. And I knew what he was doing also - did he get the same feeling after he'd been on a job like I was feeling now? He was the first real relationship I'd gotten into for years and I wanted this to work, but something didn't feel quite right. I figured that now was the time that we would need a sit down and a talk.

Café Nero, Soho.

Juan had just called, my phone showing he was calling from his home phone. Juan, some friends and I had gone to the theatre two nights ago and he managed to lose his mobile phone. I had since received a call from the police station telling me they had found it and mine had been the last number dialled (in Juan's world that was an honour). Today we were going to collect it from the station.

Typically though, Juan was calling to tell me he was going to be late. I'd just drained my hot chocolate and was left sitting in the coffee shop with nothing else to do but sit and wait, looking like a rent boy. Ok, bad analogy, but I was left to sit there like a spare part while he took his time getting there. Someone had left a copy of *Boyz* magazine on the table beside me, so I dragged it over, not realising that cold coffee was rolling off the front page and onto my leg. As I mopped the spill up with a napkin, I scanned the mag; this week's front page was adorned by three hilariously over-done drag queens wearing more sparkle than 50 Cent, Eminem and P Diddy combined. They were chinking their glasses and the headline read "Cheers, queers" - gay journalism at its finest.

I pulled out my iPod and let the Pet Shop Boys cheer me up. Truth be told, I did need cheering up. Dylan and I had met for a chat last night but for some reason he hadn't seen where I was coming from – all I'd done was ask if he had ever considered quitting his job and doing something else with his life. I'd told him that it was getting harder for me and I had entertained the idea of moving on, and then blurted out that I found it difficult to cement a relationship when I knew that he was out with other men. He argued that I knew what I was getting myself in for, and that I needed to have patience with him as he had a plan. I had scoffed at him and asked what sort of plan you needed to shove your dick into someone. The night didn't get any better from there.

Six songs later, the Pet Shop Boys had done little to improve my mood, but thankfully Juan had arrived and was tugging at my sleeve.

"Ok, ok!" I said getting up.

Among a few apologies and a quick catch-up, we made our way out of the coffee shop and I tried to ask him if he thought I was being stupid about Dylan and the whole situation – he said that I was.

The walk to Charing Cross Police Station wasn't too far and before too long we were inside the station, waiting for an officer to assist us. Juan kept fidgeting with his Commes des Garcons satchel, making me nervous. Even though I had done nothing wrong, I felt jittery and was worried I would be arrested – I stupidly relayed this to Juan who peered at me and said that judging by the way I was dressed, nothing was out of the question. A cute copper then approached and in a quiet yet forceful voice asked, "Mr Constantine?" He was nothing short of divine; tall, stocky, broad shouldered and handsome. For a moment we just sat there and gawped at him. I almost wished I had committed a crime so he could've roughed me up in one of the interview rooms. Then Juan remembered why he was there and stood up, nodding solemnly as if he were in some courtroom drama. He was a fine one to poke fun at my dress sense – he was sporting purple snakeskin trousers, pale green pullover and cravat; though it wasn't even close to the plumage and sequins he was dollied up in on Saturday night at the theatre.

I felt sorry for the policeman – he must've thought Juan was a right weirdo. Even worse, he must've thought I was his boyfriend. He introduced himself as Constable Damon Green and asks Juan to follow him to a room just a few feet from the front desk. As they walked, Constable Green hesitated, turned to me and asked me if I would like to come along as well, to which I leapt out of my chair and joined them.

Inside Interview Room 2, we were seated at a small table and offered a hot drink. Juan was still in his BAFTA mode and simply waved his hand to signal his refusal.

"Right then, er, sir. Is this your phone? We found it upon a homeless gentleman along the Charing Cross Road. Would you have any idea how it became in his possession? If it was stolen, we will need you to make a statement and we will press charges if necessary."

Juan reached across the table and took the phone, holding it up to scrutinise it, knowing full well it was his and just putting on a show for the constable. He then pulled it to his chest with his eyes closed. Constable Green looked across to me and I shrugged, signalling that I knew Juan was a little over the top and all he needed do was ride it out.

"In your own time sir" said Constable Green, smiling.

"I think it's mine, it looks like mine. I wonder officer, could you come and help me with the buttons, it's complicated and I really don't understand it. It needs a real man's touch." I rolled my eyes. *Here we go.*

"It's yours!!" I snapped, irritated that he was trying to flirt with my, I mean, the constable.

He then conceded and told Constable Green that the phone did belong to him, while shooting me a sideways glare.

"Sir, from the description of the contacts in here and what you have said, I believe this to be your phone, We now need to get to the bottom of the situation of how it ended up with this homeless gentleman" replied Constable Green, obviously enjoying this dramatic episode between Juan and I.

Juan turned to me saying that he was too upset to speak and would I be able to explain what happened, then he started texting someone.

"Can you not wait for three minutes until we're outside before you line up your next fuck" I whispered harshly in his ear. He waved me away and carries on typing.

Constable Green didn't really seem to be bothered in Juan's problem. If I'm honest, he had been stealing little glances at me since I'd sat down, although I thought all men did that to me. I turned to the officer and started to tell him of Saturday night's events and as I started, he got out his little notebook.

"Well, let's see. How did this all begin? I suppose I could blame bad parenting, but let's just fast forward to last Saturday night" I said looking purposefully at Juan who wasn't paying attention. "We went out to the theatre together with some friends and maybe we had a little too much champagne during the interval" I began. Constable Green let his mouth curl up into a tiny smile - damn, he was hot. "Oh yes, well I recall after the show we walked through Leicester Square and made our way to Compton Street....er, to go to a very plain bar where nothing exciting happened." At that point, Juan cut in, obviously not realising I was trying to paint a nicer, straighter picture to spare the officers blushes.

"No, we went to Cruise Central and you had too many beers – that fat old man wanted to grope you and I got off with the builder – how can you forget that?!" he said, quickly going back to his text message. I paused. Ok, if he didn't know we were gay before, then he surely did now. I smiled sweetly and continued.

"Thank you Juan" I said firmly "oh yes, I recall it now – so at…the bar, we had a few drinks and then Juan asked for his phone - our friend Rosie was looking after it because Juan's corset had no pockets.

"Corset?" Constable Green said, as he stopped taking notes and queried me.

"Mm-hmm, yes" I said and carried on as if there was nothing amiss, "so anyway, Rosie was a bit drunk and had been practically accosting every man in sight, reached for the phone, but couldn't find it."

"So Rosie lost the phone then? And who is she?" Constable Green asked.

"Er, well, *he* was the guy we went to the theatre with – we got changed at his place."

"He..?"

"Yeah, Rosie – is a bloke. Well, his real name is Robert. But we called him Rosie."

The amusement had left the constable's face, to be replaced with a look of concern.

"So, we reckoned the phone has probably fallen through a hole in one of Rosie's fishnets, so decided to backtrack and look for it."

"He was wearing fishnet stockings?

"Yeah, well luckily they were hold-ups, because he snapped the suspender belt after the lady behind the merchandise stall really tugged at it to get him off the poor usher who he was trying to get off with. I was surprised they didn't throw us out come to think of it." Constable Green said nothing, he just scribbled in his pad. "So yeah, we walked and walked to find this goddamn phone, but I had to stop because my feet were killing as my stilettos are a size too small – "

"Stilettos?" Constable Green nearly dropped his pen and looked a little more startled.

"Yeah, I was dressed as the maid".

All that met me from Constable Green was a blank stare. I misunderstood his silence as of one of non-comprehension, so I elaborated.

"You know, one of those French numbers…little black dress, stilettos, fishnets and a tiny frilly apron and hat to match".

Constable Green took a deep breath and soldiered on. "May I ask what show you saw…just so I can confirm times, etc."

"Well, this is the thing you see. Our plan for that night was to get dollied up and go off to a sing-a-long Rocky Horror show" I said, starting to stumble over my words. The more that Constable Green stared at me, the faster I spoke. The rest came out in a frantic rush. "Rosie had planned all the tickets and we were to pay him back when we arrived. Rosie assured us everything was okay as he had booked everything online, all we needed to do was pick up the tickets at the box office. I wasn't sure what the mix-up was, but apparently Rosie wasn't too good with internet bookings. Well he was good at buying porn, but that's another matter. Anyway, we ended up at the Royal Opera House watching *La Bohème*. I tell you, those seats really weren't comfortable at all…and the woman behind me had the audacity to ask me to take my wig off as she couldn't see."

I took a deep breath, exhaled and smiled at Constable Green.

"Ah…okay" he noted; now with his head bent so low to the desk I couldn't see his face at all. I think he was pretending to write intensely, but I could tell from the shaking that he was now in silent hysterics.

Thankfully Juan had come back to his senses. He had stopped texting; clearly he had finished lining up work for the next week.

Ten minutes later, we were walking back to Soho after I had given Constable Green the statement, along with my phone number. I thought that he would appreciate having such a good ending to a story he was no doubt telling the rest of the station upon our exit.

Bermondsey, South London.

Juan had invited me to his friend Christo's for dinner. At first I was a little reluctant because Christo was one of the new movement of New Age-preaching, lactose-spurning, linen-wearing, buckwheat-toting homosexuals. He had a passion for loving and maintaining the planet, even though he managed to bring most of it back with him to adorn various coffee tables and shelves around his home. A spindly, wiry and earthy lad who was very at one with nature, he was often dressed in something made of muslin. He would often jet around the world at the expense of his long term lover/sugar daddy, while said lover/sugar daddy was playing real daddy to Isabella and Toby, and managed a complex marriage with a beautiful wife called Linda somewhere in Hampstead.

There wasn't a rainforest or a mountain in the whole of Asia that Christo hadn't delved into or scaled. He was something of a selective naturalist though – he couldn't stand being dirty or unclean, and was constantly drenching himself in designer fragrances and scrubbing himself with luxurious bubbling bath oils and loofahs. His travel bag usually held Imodium, Tiger Balm and something by Jean Paul Gaultier.

When confronted by a friend of Juan's that he was being hypocritical as most of the products he used were contributing to the ever-declining natural world and ever-increasing ozone layer problems, he spouted that he could still love the planet and cherish all of God's creations while still being able to undertake good grooming and not smell like the bottom of a skip.

To be honest, I was dreading the evening and would have said no if I actually had a valid reason, which I didn't. However, Juan had cornered me with the "what are you doing tonight" question. Before I had a chance to think of something, I was invited. I could just see how it would all unfold - a dinner of lentil stew and soya bean pâté followed by a slideshow of Christo trekking through the depths of Borneo in his Vivien Westwood mules.

Then again, it was probably good that I was out; Dylan was working again and I didn't really want to sit at home playing Patty Paranoia.

As slide 43 came up on screen, I heaved a sigh, loudly enough that one of Christo's friends to turned to me and tutted. Christo gushed again. "This was such a humbling experience you guys, it really made me appreciate that the most precious, natural and beautiful things in life are free, you know?" he said as he stood before his huge wall-sized projector in the dimly lit dining room. "And my hi-def camcorder worked a treat for zooming in on the rare Asian pigmy-toed, hunchback red-backed Marmosets!" he squealed.

I sat there dry-chewing my mung-bean and turnip canapés while he delved into the history of the paper-bark tree – his part-time lover sashaying around making sure that everyone was topped up with their elderflower juice. I wondered what Linda and the kids in Hampstead were doing tonight.

The next few slides showed a mixture of forests and streams before Christo stopped to tell us all about his adventure of hiring a guide who demanded he be paid two pounds for his time. Laughing, he pointed out that rather than pay the money, he did that particular trek alone and took a self portrait. After his introduction, a giant image of Christo was projected onto the wall, showing him mid-climb up a giant tree with his Versace satchel swinging behind him. I let out another sigh, unsure how much of this evening I would be able to stand.

After a good hour of slides and garden weeds on toast, he decided we should sit in the drawing room and relax. Excellent – I was really in the mood for a big, fat coffee and a few hours of trashy telly. However, his idea of relaxing was to sit cross-legged on the Hessian flooring by a cluster of church candles, desperately trying to fold himself into some kind of lotus flower or something, while inhaling the sickly sent of a variation of incenses.

I'm not adverse to incense, and burning one at a time, I usually enjoy it. However, the lethal combination of Sandalwood, Lavender, Primrose and Juniper fumes spewing out of the incense holders were making me a little light headed - or it could have been the turnip platter. He had also put a few herbal remedy sticks in to burn as well, though I'm not sure any medical establishment had ever passed them as safe.

The evening trailed on and Juan sat cross-legged on the floor near Christo as if he was some temple-worshipping enthusiast; eyes closed and a look of concentration on his face. It took me quite by surprise as I had expected Juan to give him a big mouthful, dismissing his beliefs as a load of shit, before lighting up a cone. I then spotted his iPod was plugged in and realised that even he had enough of Christo's incessant droning.

Around 9pm, I checked my phone for missed calls or messages from Dylan – there were none. Perhaps he was still working? Perhaps he left his phone at home? Perhaps he just wasn't thinking about me? I was sitting there in my own trance-like state, quite comfortable to tune out, until I realised that the two dreadlocked lesbians who had joined us for dinner were unbuttoning their hemp shirts. It seemed that to really feel the power of the universe and all of its pumpkin seeds, one must get ones breasts out.

The high point of my evening finally came, when Christo decided to burn some sage to cleanse the air of impurities and bad omens. Crouching by a small, walnut mantle he carefully lit a bundle of sage and when it started to chug smoke he began waving it around, dotting at the air and around himself. However, after a vigorous cleansing movement with the burning herb, he succeeded in setting light to his linen head wrap and spent the rest of the night swearing like a fishwife and maintaining that he was through with nature – that was satisfying enough for me and I was actually glad I made the effort to go.

After a great debrief out the front of Christo's with Juan amidst a fit of giggles, we walked and laughed back to the station. I gave him a few air kisses, "One shouldn't connect, Rich, it ruins the whole pretence of air kissing", at Victoria station and then decided I would go for a walk. I was having real problems coping at the moment…perhaps incense was only for small doses.

As I came out of the station, I pulled out my phone to see if Dylan had texted me. Of course all I had done since last checking it was to walk Juan to the entrance of the northbound Victoria line and exit the station, but there was actually a message. I stared at the little envelope on my phone and was almost too nervous to press the 'read' button.

I decided then and there that if Dylan truly wanted me and was committed to investing fully in our relationship he would text me. Oh who was I kidding? Who wanted to be with someone who obsessed as much as I did and checked his phone every two minutes to see if his boyfriend…

"Excuse me?"

I turned around and standing before me was an elderly lady dressed in brown trousers, a tweed jacket and peaked cap. She looked like she had just stepped off the cover of the Horse & Hound magazine. Perhaps this was where the country folk stayed when they came to protest their right to annihilate foxes with their oversized guns.

"Can I help you?" I asked, hoping that she wasn't going to ask me to help her across the road, or worse still – open her bottle of gin or whatever that was in the brown paper bag she was clutching.

"Are you okay? I don't usually interfere, but you seem a little dazed and you're talking to yourself" she said

I stared at her for a second, alarmed that I had actually been conversing with myself out loud, then smiled. "Oh, sorry, no it's fine, yes I'm perfectly fine, well, a little fine – but ever so slightly schizoid, you never know what I'm capable of" I whispered, meaning it as a joke, but she failed to get my humour practically ran away from me.

I walked off briskly towards the Palace in a hurry, hoping to get away from the crowded station.

"Ok, so I've lost the ability to have an inner monologue, nothing wrong with that, probably just under a little duress – or it's the bloody incense –I'm tripping out on it.....I'm...I'm.....doing it again, I'm still chatting to myself. Why do I need to be talking out loud....and why am I even asking myself?"

I remembered my phone and checked the message. It was from Dylan. All it said was "@ hotel 2200 in Vic. c u l8r if ur awke".

Hotel Twenty200 in Victoria, that was just around the corner. Well, it would've been rude not to stop by to see how things were going. I hoped that the walk would clear my head and I would be a little less scattered when I arrived, but the hotel was actually only a couple of hundred metres from the station. In no time at all, I was standing in the lobby and force of habit had brought me to the lobby where a rather large man waited behind the reception.

"Can I help you sir" the night manager asked. I glanced down to see his name badge; Filip. What sort of dumb way is that to spell...? I stopped myself half way through my thought just in case I was saying it out loud. He stared at me strangely when I hadn't answered him.

"Why hello" I began, not really knowing where I was going with my words. "I'm looking for my...friend; Dylan." I didn't say boyfriend, just because some people still had a problem with that sort of thing.

"Last name please, sir" he said, as his fingers poised over the keys of his computer behind the desk. Oh holy God – I couldn't remember it. It felt like I was tweaking on whatever it was at Christo's. Come to think of it, for all I knew, Dylan might not even been his real name. I really felt like an idiot as Filip was looking at me expectedly.

"It's just Dylan, you know, like Cher" I soldiered on looking around hoping that I could get through this. I closed my eyes and open them again, trying to focus; suddenly realising I was feeling quite out of it. "Wooooh, I'm really fucked up on that goddamn incense."

"I beg your pardon sir?" Filip said, moving away from the keyboard, placing his hands on the counter.

God I did it again…

"Sorry it's nothing – he must not have checked in yet. I have a business meeting with him so I'll just wait over there". Nice one Rich, a business meeting at 11:30pm on a Tuesday night, perfect.

I sat on the couch near the elevators, grabbing a magazine from the coffee table and buried myself in Home and Garden for fifteen minutes, well aware that Filip was casting disparaging looks my way. I finally realised that I was being an idiot and decided to get up and leave, though not before finishing a thoroughly life changing story about family in Camden who changed from Parquet flooring to slate. As I threw the magazine back on the table, I glance again to Filip, rolling my eyes and pointing to my watch, keeping up the whole business meeting façade. Just before I could reach the exit, the lift behind me chimed; lo and behold; Dylan strutted out, closely followed by Mark.

Shit… shit, shit, shit. In a desperate bid to act cool, calm and collected, I darted behind an oversized potted fern. I didn't think they saw me, but

Filip might have noticed – oh who cared about him anyway. What the fuck was I going to do? If I stepped out now, Dylan would think that I'd been here all night, stalking him. Then again, if I hid there any longer they would both have to pass me soon enough and then how would I explain to them that I was hiding in the shrubbery? I decided to stay there, shrinking into myself as much as I could and hoping for the best. Dylan and Mark were at the counter; Mark looked to be settling the bill while Dylan was fiddling with his phone. He must have said something vaguely amusing because Dylan erupted in laughter, placing a hand on the small of his back. I wanted to charge over there and rip his hand off, but I stayed where I was, safely behind my pot plant. Then they turned and were about to leave - I had to stay very quiet. Just as they were about to pass me my mobile phone bleeped and Dylan looked in my direction, stepping forward to part the branches. Taking a step back he was looking at me with both eyebrows raised and a look of fear and shock upon his gorgeous face. Well, I was squatting on the floor, behind a pot plant – why wouldn't he be worried.

"Um...hello Dylan, I'm just..." I said trying to explain myself, but falling short and leaving the sentence half-finished.

"I just sent you a message – clearly you've just received it. Rich, what are you..." he said with his voice softening. Before he could complete his sentence, I cut him off.

"I'm here waiting for a friend actually. And I've not been here all night or anything. As a matter of fact, I've just got here. And when I arrived, I thought I would make it more exciting by....hiding. " I said, unconvincingly. "So, you seem to be having a nice night with *Mark*. Hi Mark, gosh it's *swell* to see you again. Well, you'd better go about your 'business' with him, and I'll stay here; friend waiting. Well go on then, shoo". Why the hell did I just say shoo?

"Rich, what's wrong?" Dylan implored.

Before I knew it, I blurted out "Well, I can now see why you don't want to give up servicing the whole of London."

"Don't be stupid Rich" Dylan said getting angry at me.

"Stupid? I'm not being stupid at all. In fact I'm being very smart, confronting you with this. Here I was, thinking that you liked me, but you're just filling in your time between *our* appointments with Mark. I don't want to be your part-time lover, so just go and be with him, you look so happy together - I hope that you two have a great life."

Mark had already left to wait outside, and a few new arrivals in the lobby as well as Filip and a nearby security officer were all looking at me. Dylan seemed unable to respond. After opening his mouth to say something, he shut it again and turning around, he stormed out.

When I was sure they had walked far enough away, I stepped out from behind the fern and dusted myself down. The security officer had retreated back behind the desk with Filip and they both looked a little worried. Quickly, I scurried out of the lobby too and exhaled deeply when I saw them both walking away in the distance. Remembering my text message I scrabbled in my bag for my phone.

'Hey babe – am fnsh wrk soon – cnt w8 2 c u – miss u. Dx'

Bugger, I'd blown it, surely, unless I was over-reacting? Maybe all was not lost. Dylan knew what I was like. He knew I got anxious sometimes. Anxious yes, deranged, no. Just as I was tucking my phone back into my bag, it beeped again. As I read the text, something inside seemed to explode into a million sharp daggers, each one embedding itself into my heart.

'Think we need 2 talk. 2nite was bit scary. Call u tomo – mite need sum time apart?'

Wednesday afternoon in my flat.

It had been a day and a half since my stupid rant in the hotel lobby and I hadn't heard from Dylan since his last text, and I hadn't really been doing anything since. I'd turned down dinner and drinks with Jacqui and Debs tonight as I couldn't face them, giving some bullshit excuse about working, but I think they knew something was up.

I could just about see my alarm clock from where I was laying; it was almost 2pm. I didn't panic about the time and I wasn't even tired, yet I pulled the covers over my head and let myself doze off in the warm darkness. I could hear my phone ringing again, but didn't bother to answer it - I let myself fall back into a sleepless sleep. When I poked my head out from under the covers again, I was hit by clean-smelling air and the feeling of space. The clock was now showing me it was 4:11pm.

I stumbled out of my bedroom and down the hall. In the living room, I fell into the sofa and curled my legs up close to me, turning on the TV. The remote didn't respond - seemed the batteries needed replacing. Rather than getting up and walking to the telly, I just pressed the buttons in harder, shaking the remote until my command was met. Paul O'Grady was glaring at me from the television but because it was muted, I couldn't hear him, but was sure he was talking about his dog; Buster who was next to him – next I was looking at a shot of the audience who were laughing. Rather than bothering with volume, I stared off into space at the wall above the telly. Why hadn't Dylan gotten in touch with me? Oh yes, I remembered, it was because I was crazy. I thought about texting him, and then told myself not to. Then I decided I should. Then I decide I shouldn't. I was half defiant that I didn't need to initiate this conversation, but the other half of me was just too frightened to inevitably start talking about our probable break up. The phone rang again and I ran to the bedroom dropping the remote as I did.

An hour or so later, I hung up and thought about what Juan had said. On the surface he came across as an uncaring, selfish person, but he really could be sensitive and considerate. Some of what he was saying though was obviously taken from a magazine or something, as he referred to me as 'dear reader' on several occasions; but his sentiment meant a lot to me nonetheless.

I thought about tidying myself up and getting ready for the day, but as it was almost six o'clock, I didn't pursue this. I folded myself back up on the sofa and let my mind go for a little run while I stared through the television set. Somehow I was thinking about how our break up conversation would go.

"We're just in different places I think" – no, too obvious.
"I don't think I'm really the settling down kind" – too bullshit.
"Rich, you're a mentalist – keep away from me" – hmm, that's probably more like it.

Oh good, at least Big Brother was on E4, lifting my spirit a little, thus cementing the fact that reality TV had been around too long and I was losing the ability to relate to anyone else without the aid of TV. Here I was, sat powerless and filled with fear about calling someone who I was totally smitten with, but could still watch eleven total strangers eat, sleep and worry about who was nominating who.

At 9:22pm a Chinese takeaway was delivered by a little fat man on a motorbike. I didn't order the chilli chicken that was in front of me now, but I ate it anyway because I was starving. In the living room, I sat on the floor and swigged from a can of beer. Draining the warming dregs, I cracked open a fresh one and shovelled food into my mouth. Still no text or call from Dylan. As I chewed I contemplated just taking this situation by the balls and calling him; I reached for my phone. Then I thought better of it and put it back down, leaving a smear of sauce on the keypad. Did I really want to salvage this relationship? Was it even breaking up? I had too many thoughts in my head and all I really cared about was that I'd forgotten to order any spring rolls. Twenty six minutes later the little fat man on the motorbike sped away again and I ripped the lid off my spring rolls munching away greedily, cooling the heat that filled my mouth by taking a big gulp of beer. It was getting on for eleven o'clock and I felt disgusted with myself. My skin was greasy and my teeth were all scummy as I hadn't made any attempt to cleanse myself today. I hadn't even had a wee or anything; even my body was giving up on me too. In the bathroom I scrabbled for the light pull and blinked a few times as it sparked to life. I had been sitting in the darkness, my only source of light from the television, for five hours now – I was shameful. Looking in the mirror, I didn't recognise the man who looking back at me: my hair was flat and had parted itself in the centre, my eyes were bloodshot and puffy looking, I had two days stubble dotted over my lower face and my skin had a jaundice look to it, which I hoped was due to the dingy light bulb I had in my bathroom. That was also the first time I really took notice in what I was wearing: red tracksuit bottoms with a hole in one leg and a nasty, brown knitted sweater that was stretched out of shape from too many washes.

I was thoroughly ashamed of myself for a minute, but then realised I was going through an emotionally difficult time right now; I was being too hard on myself. I was more often than not perky and cheerful; my friends rarely saw a side of me looking like this. I deserved to wallow in self-pity and misery – and ugly clothing.

I stared at myself for a while before taking a deep breath and letting it out in a sigh. Sure, I had been pretty patient with myself and letting my blue mood take me down into a spiral of beer and takeaways but I really had to get over this. Instantly I changed my thinking and decided that tomorrow I would wake up early and scrub myself clean. Then I would go to the gym for two or three hours, then follow this with a swim and treat myself to a super healthy lunch. Dylan did not rule my life, he was just a man. I thought back to the old adage that I desperately hated about fish in the sea and I made myself believe I would go fishing tomorrow.

"I am taking back my life" I said out loud, feeling good. Then I looked at my reflection again and was brought crashing down.

Twenty two minutes later, the little fat man was once again speeding away on his bike. I stood in the kitchen eating pineapple fritters with a plastic fork. They must have felt sorry for me at the Chinese restaurant because there were some fortune cookies that have been thrown in for free. I cracked one open: *The wealthy man will have a poor existence.* What does that even mean? I cracked another: *Belief is merely the hope of foolery and misconception.* I smashed the last with my fist, angrily: *Love is blind.* Looking down at myself, I realised the only way Dylan would ever want to be with me again was if he *was* blind.

12:47am and still no call or text from Dylan. Now I was just angry, he wasn't even thinking about me enough to get in touch. Without realising it, I checked my inbox and scrolled to each of his messages. I remembered receiving each one and how good they made me feel. Then I flicked from my inbox to my sent messages and then back and forth, re-living the conversation as it happened. As I read I realised Dylan was worth fighting for. I had been stupid, I didn't want to lose him, or let him think that I wasn't bothered about him. I decided to call, I had to! It was my fault he was freaked out in the first place - I should have done it last night, what an idiot I was!

I dialled his number, feeling quite calm waiting for him to answer with his trademark "Yo, it's Dylan" response. He didn't. The phone rang and rang; it seemed to ring for a long time before I was re-routed to his mailbox. In the few short seconds before the voicemail kicked in I wondered if I should have hung up. "Yo – this is Dylan – I can't speak to you at the mo, but leave a message and I'll get right back to you…cheers!" The tone beeped and I froze up, paralysed and unable to speak. I had been silent for about five seconds, I had to say something!

"Hey….hey Dylan – it's me – Rich. Hey. Erm, I just wanted to call you for a chat – but you must be busy, or maybe asleep. Or, or maybe you're not even there, which is odd because if you have a mobile phone then the chances are it would be with you, I mean, that's why it's called a mobile……" Panic set in, I was burning up – get to the point, I told myself angrily. "anyway, as I said, I er, thought I should call to explain – er, but you're not there are you. Ok – well, hey, give me a call or a text when you're free and we can have a chat. It's Rich by the way. Oh I said that already."

My voice trailed off hopelessly as I put the phone down, instantly forgetting everything I had just said. Did I get my point across that I wanted to speak to him? Maybe I just rambled on – I didn't want him to think I was any more of a nutjob than he already did. I did the only sensible thing I could and followed up my call by texting him. After my allocated 160 characters, I was satisfied that I had now made a valid attempt to clear my thinking and restore his faith in me as a normal boyfriend. After pacing around the lounge room a few more times, I decided to go to bed - but not before finishing the pineapple fritters.

I woke around 2:20; my phone beeping at me with a message. Squinting in the dark my heart froze and my fingers seized up so that I couldn't open it. It was from Dylan. Regaining my composure, I selected OK and read it, but was left feeling sick and confused.

"Rich – dnt think u shd contact me 4 while – sorry, will call soon – need time 4 me."

What is he talking about, why shouldn't I contact him? Suddenly I remembered that I sent a text. I raced to my sent messages and shook my head as I read my epic message.

"Hey baby, missing u – I no u mite b upset but cum over and we can talk. Or I can cum to u. Or ill call u again. Or I can text u again later? Y haven't u called?"

In the space of a few days I had well and truly fucked up this relationship.

I. Am. Mental.

Friday, 2 Weeks AD (After-Dylan) – South Wimbledon.

"Little Miss Muffet?" shouted Debs from the betting booth.

"Yeah, gimme some muff" I yelled back, slopping beer out of my plastic cup and down my Paul Smith shirt. "Bollocks" I added, wiping the beer across my chest, enlarging the wet patch.

Jacqui was yelling obscenities at her greyhound as it went rushing by the fence, madly running around the track after the mechanical rabbit. The dog was coming dead last and it had Jacqui's last tenner on it. I looked out over the track, taking stock of my situation. Two weeks ago I was madly happy, running around Hyde Park with my man in his-and-his tracksuits while other men looked on with envy. Now I was chugging beer out of a plastic cup watching dog racing with south London's crème de la crème, getting leered at by small, toothless bookies with Brylcreem hairdos. While scanning the crowd looking for some talent, I caught sight of an older women stumbling around. She was dressed in a figure-hugging, cheetah-print jumpsuit; her hair was teased and piled up on her head and held in place with some severe looking clips. As she limped past, sucking on a cigarette, I looked down and noticed one of her heels has snapped off her shoes. Socially, I had hit rock bottom.

Debs bounded back with the betting slip and thrusted it into my hand – there, written in large print was "Little Miss Muffet 10-1". I looked up at her and started to laugh. For all the problems of having a relationship go south, at least I had great friends. In fact it was Debs that gotten me out of my fortnight of spiralling depression with a quick phone call. I had awoken to the sound of the phone ringing earlier today - I would like to say earlier this morning right after my jog, but truth be told, I hadn't been getting out of bed before lunchtime since I was dumped.

I had pulled myself off the rug near the electric heater in the lounge room — where I had fallen into a drunken stupor the night before, and dragged my sorry arse over to the phone. I tried to mumble a greeting, acutely aware of my hideous morning-after breath, when a shrill voice was already blasting at me.

"Where the fuck've you been?" Debs tore into me without giving me time to respond "what, you're too good now you have a boyfriend to pick up the fucking phone? Honestly, you treat us like we're second rate citizens now. When was the last time you bothered to catch up with us, I mean, God, it's not like we can just be put on a shelf until you're ready for us. Oh, and another thing…"

"We broke up" I blurted out. I didn't really want to tell her but I didn't know what else to say to stop her yelling. As soon as I'd said it, it really hit home that it was truth and I was alone again. Then I started to cry.

"Oh….fuck….I'm sorry Rich, you know I was shitty coz I love you and I miss hanging out with you. What happened? Actually — don't tell me yet, I'm coming over — put the kettle on."

Three tube stops and a brisk walk from the station later and she was at my door; in the same time I had only managed to rub the carpet fluff from my face and walk to the kitchen, where I had been vacantly opening and closing the same three cupboard doors looking for the Nescafe.

Debs didn't wait for me to answer the door and came in the front entrance and up the stairs. As she stood in my flat's doorway she looked around at the mess that was once my home. If I had been in any emotional state to care, I would have been totally ashamed of my surroundings. What was once a clean, minimalist apartment had now become a university-style student shit-hole; clothes all over the floor, empty cake boxes on the mantle, crushed cans of beer on the floor.

"Oh Rich…what happened? Don't tell me you were you broken into as well!" She looked appalled as she stepped over a small pile of dirty pants. I had been sorting my laundry by rooms, the front hall being reserved for underwear. Before I could say anything, she came into the kitchen and saw me standing in my Tikka Masala-stained bathrobe.

She hugged me tightly, holding me close and stroking my hair. After having my cry on the phone (and for a few minutes after I had hung up) I felt emotionally numb. I hadn't had any clients since Dylan had broken up with me, and had spent the past two weeks pottering around in my pants and feeling sorry for myself.

"Right, into the shower with you, you smell like cat vomit. I'll take care of stuff out here". Typical Debs, functional right down to the last. I dragged myself off to the bathroom, stripped off and stepped under the hot water, letting it wash over me. I lost track of the time as I scrubbed myself clean, indulging in all my favourite over-priced products: face wash, body wash, shampoo, toner, body polish. After not bathing for almost a week, I felt I deserved a ridiculously long shower. I towel-dried my hair and wrapped myself up in a waffle bathrobe Juan had stolen for me as a gift from a holiday in Singapore. I stepped out of the bathroom, through my flat-cum-walk-in wardrobe and into my bedroom. Bless!

Debs had made my bed and thrown all the dirty clothes into the hamper – well, in and next to the hamper, considering there was nearly three weeks of it strewn throughout the place. I threw on some of my nicer clothes and strode out to the kitchen, feeling better already.

"Hey beautiful" I heard as I approached the kitchen. Sitting in the lounge room was Jacqui. "What the…when did you get here?" I stammered.

"Funnily enough, I was driving home from my hairdressers when Debs called half an hour ago, so I swung by…I even had enough time to get those" grinned Jaqs, pointing to a couple of bottles of Absolut sitting on the bench. I jumped on her, giving her a tight hug.

Debs had managed to clean up three quarters of the apartment in my short absence, obviously confirming her status as the most anal of the three of us. An hour later we were all laughing hysterically as I told them of my dinner at Christo's house and trying to hide from Dylan in a shrub at the hotel. It was quite a healing process being able to talk to them and finally laugh about the whole situation.

"Fuck 'im" slurred Debs as she emptied the second bottle of vodka to top up her drink. "Fuck em allllll…I reckon that you…" she emphasised as she threw her arms out wide, "arejustfuckingperfect."

"I've got a great idea" shouted Jaqs, interrupting Debs' pissed rant. The three of us talk over each other most of the time, but when drunk, we all just shout out our conversation to be heard. Jaqs stood up and declared herself.

"Grab your coats girls…we're off to Wimbledon."

Sunday morning in my flat.

I had recently returned home after treating myself to a last minute holiday in Majorca – I felt I needed a break and some sunshine. The whole thing was a bloody bargain if I do say so myself: £190 all inclusive. I got it right at the last minute, packed the bare essentials and slept, swam and suntanned my week away and indulging in some wonderful me-time. I had purposely left my phone in London and didn't think once about work or what was waiting for me back home. Now that I was feeling more refreshed, and it had been over a month since the whole relationship meltdown, I was picking myself up again. I hadn't worked in that time and I wasn't missing it at all. Id had some cash stashed away in case of a rainy day and that last month had been a definite Noah's Ark situation.

Sitting against my couch, I let the morning sunshine wash over me as I sipped on my espresso. I had missed getting up early - well, 10am. I flicked through the newspaper on the floor next to me to see what was going on in London this week. I had always found the magazines to be far more interesting and colourful than the actual newspaper itself, plus, one didn't need a wet-wipe after reading them.

My options weren't exactly abundant; jazz tomorrow night in Soho, perhaps Salsa lessons on Tottenham Court road on Tuesday. I closed the paper and swapped it for copy of Gay Times I had bought a few months back, forgetting to toss it out and buy a new one. I never really read it cover to cover – just flicked through it scanning the pages for pretty people and the star signs. I opened it at random to the classifieds. I used to read through these with a friend a few years back, laughing at the preposterous adverts we found. 'Virile hung stud with xpnse acct lookin 4 boy to spoil': translation – old impotent fucker with pencil dick and twenty pounds. I read further and stopped at one halfway down the page; 'Fat, bald and desperate'. Oh my God, I had just seen my future. Quickly moving on to see what else I could find I was actually enjoying them. It seemed there were loads of guys out there waiting for a date. Maybe this could be a good idea, I mean I didn't have to date all of them - I could find a few good ones that would maybe consider hooking up with me regularly.

I sat there lying to myself that this could be good for my business; all the while secretly hoping this would be a way to find Mr Right. For the next half an hour, I tried to come up with a sufficient summary of who I was within twenty-five words; any more would cost extra and that would have been a waste of money. Being so miserly though, it was getting hard to summarise myself in such a small space; trying to define oneself and ones finer points was all well and good, but with all abbreviating I had come up with little more than a glorified eye chart. On my fourth attempt, I thought that I had nailed it.

'Good looking, twenty something lad from Victoria WLTM TDH lad for fun, friendship and poss LTR. Sincere and very normal – what are you waiting for?'

I picked up the phone and placed my advert, relying once again on those nice people at MasterCard. As I set the receiver back in its cradle, I wondered if I had done the right thing or if I was just walking right into another disaster. Either way, it was too late now, and I might not even get any responses. I finished my espresso and sank into the sofa, reading the rest of the magazine until I read something utterly shocking: you could actually date people via the television! I read the advert again to make sure I wasn't hallucinating. I wasn't – the process seemed quite simple – you paid your money, went to a certain bar on the dates given, and you had to record a video message that would beamed out on a dating channel. Oh this was just too weird, but my mind started ticking and I was quickly seduced by the idea of it, feeling half ashamed and half curious. Surely it was a desperate attempt to flag down any single passing person in the lure of love and happiness – but maybe it couldn't do that much harm to really make sure you are out there. It was like good PR I supposed. I wouldn't do anything about it now; maybe I'd carefully raise the subject with some friends to get their verdict. If they collapsed in a heap of giggles, I'd know not to go along with it. If they were supportive and pro-active, I would go for it. I thought about Juan, Debs, Jacqui and some of my other good friends, and could guess their reactions. Deciding not to tell any of them, I had to find someone who would appreciate it and not laugh it off as desperation. I needed to find someone more tragic than me – bingo; Jane who I used to go to school with. We had kept in touch on and off since year 9.

She wasn't totally tragic, but she was over the halfway mark for sure - the only social occasion she regularly attended was her daily journey to and from work. I had tried inviting her out with me on numerous occasions but she always pulled out at the last minute. I knew she was desperate for a boyfriend as well, or even any male attention - the fact that UPS no longer delivered to her door for signed goods was only testament to this. I wasted no time in calling her.

Later that week I found myself sitting awkwardly in Jane's mother's front room, waiting for her to finish getting ready upstairs.

"No thank you Mrs Quinn" I said as Jane's mum offered me a fourth slice of Battenberg. She clearly still thought I was a teenager. I could hear Jane stomping about upstairs, getting ready. I knew she was excited; she was playing her getting ready music. Sadly, Jane thought she was still a teenager; Bros was playing loudly through the floorboards into the dated living room where I sat.

"So, are you courting" asks Mrs Quinn "anyone special in mind, any nice young ladies?"

Oh Jesus. Well, there was no need for me to launch into the history of my sexuality now, so I decided to just placate her and tell her that I was single, which wasn't a lie.

"Jane is such a nice girl, but then, you know that don't you dear?" I could guess were this might be heading. "And she's such a clever girl. Did you know she recently got a promotion?" I widened my eyes to show some interest and Mrs Quinn carried on talking, gently rubbing the sides of her coffee mug between her hands as she did. "Yes, she's had a pay rise and can now be left unattended. As long as she promises not to touch the animals" she quickly added.

When Jane left school, or more to the point was asked to leave, she got a job as a veterinary nurse with the RSPCA. The thing was the position wasn't quite real as the real staff had only made it up because she used to spend all her free time volunteering for them. They felt it only right they should pay her back somehow – especially as no-one else seemed too keen to employ her. Obviously she wasn't allowed to carry out or take part in any surgeries that took place – she was more of a silent helper – emptying bins, stuffing envelopes – that kind of thing.

"Yes, she's very happy now." Mrs Quinn carried on. Silence followed and fell over us both, parted only by the ticking of the hideously over-lacquered carriage clock by the window. After a lengthy and very awkward silence, Mrs Quinn soldiered on, apparently allergic to silence. "Of course, she's still looking for that special someone." I rolled my eyes as she looked down to her cup. Thankfully, before she could pipe up again, Jane screamed out loudly, giving me an exit.

"I think I'll just go and see if she needs any help getting ready" I said, Mrs Quinn looking me up and down probably sizing me up for wedding attire.

Upstairs, I found Jane in her room, sitting on the floor and sobbing with her back to me. As I walked in, I turned the volume down on her hot pink stereo and accidentally knocked a stack of cassette boxes to the floor. Clothes were strewn all over the place, on the floor, on the bed, and pungent perfume which smelt like bleach was lingering in the air. As she turned to me I could see she had scalded her forehead with her ceramic hair tongs and now had a reddening streak joining her hairline to her eyebrow. After drying her eyes and having another piece of Battenberg each, I helped her pick out something vaguely pretty while we discussed school life and the things we used to talk about back in the day; it was hard to have a current conversation with her because we so very rarely saw each other - it was like regression therapy but a lot cheaper. Finally we left the house and made our way to Trinity nightclub. Rather than letting her daughter have any semblance of independence, Mrs Quinn insisted on driving us into town. On the way, Jane talked non-stop about her promotion and how excited she was to be in such a fulfilling job. My eyes glazed over as we headed into town and I felt bad that I was blatantly using her because my real friends had too much integrity to come with me instead. For Jane it though, it was an adventure she rarely had – going out into town with a friend.

We were dropped by the front of the bustling nightclub and as we walked away from the orange Volvo, Mrs Quinn yelled out that she would be back to pick us both up at 11pm. I cringed and tried to pretend I wasn't with them.

As we finally stepped into the club, I felt a little less embarrassed about the whole evening. Jane settled into a booth while I got the drinks in and something told me this was going to be one of those nights, heavily reliant on alcohol. I sipped at my glass of wine while she chugged on her third bottle of Diamond White, and again we struggled with any conversation outside of small talk about school until we finally plucked up the courage to approach the film crew who had been setting up in the far corner. A poncey-looking man with a jumper thrown over his shoulders was mincing about and pointing to people randomly, while a gaggle of runners propped up lights and fiddled with wires, oblivious to his direction. A small group of desperados had been rounded up and were waiting to record their messages; so we sat and watched for a while just to get the feel of it. It didn't look too bad actually; someone seated himself at the 'love booth', which was just a big red chair, and he spoke about himself for a few minutes. All the other people waiting to have a go had a number pinned to their chest and all had one thing in common; they looked mortified. Ironically, I was actually quite excited about having a go and I started running through what I was going to say. I turned to Jane to offer her another keg but she had made a mad dash for the love booth and was next in line. I moved a bit closer, quite frightened to watch her. She looked over to me and waved wildly, bless her, she looked like a big potato in a cardigan. The director was talking to her and when she finished waving and giggling like a reprobate, she looked blankly at him while sucking her drink through a straw.

"Just tell us your name, love, and then the type of person you like, love, and just be bubbly love, bubbly." With a clap of his hands, the poncey-looking man retreated back to his cameraman as if he is some big shot director on a Hollywood blockbuster. "Action love, action."

Jane looked petrified; the red welt on her forehead seemed to be throbbing and her sallow cheeks had a quiver to them. As she opened her mouth to speak I could see she had lipstick smeared over her teeth.

"JANE" she declared loudly.

The poncey-looking man poked his head up from the camera and signalled with his hand for her to carry on. After a short pause she went into auto-ramble, obviously gaining confidence as she did. By the time her ordeal was over she looked out of breath and drained and we met up again at the bar where she sucked desperately on a bottle of beer, asking me how it looked. Carefully choosing some choice words, I congratulated her on a fine performance.

"It was ok, you're sure?"

I thought hard and decided not to mention all the things she really shouldn't have talked about; her pet rabbit, her accident with the hair tongs, her psoriasis.

"You did fine mate" I told her as I drained my wine.

"You're up next I think, go join the queue, go on" she said with a forceful push. Now, by contrast, I had cold feet but couldn't back out - after all, it was my idea to do this. After her interview it seemed Jane had scared most of the people from the queue, myself included. Even before I was near the love booth, the guy in charge came bounding up, preparing to pin a number to my shirt.

"Oh my, you *have* to do this. People as good looking as you usually don't do this..." he simpered, obviously trying to sweet-talk me, but only resulting in making me more afraid and self-conscious. As I took my seat I couldn't help but wonder how many buttocks of sad, lonely losers had sat here before me. Some passers-by were milling around with their designer beers, whispering to each other and looking at me, doing exactly what I had just done to Jane. I puffed myself up and gave my hair a bit of a tussle. Number 711 was pinned to my chest; somehow I didn't think this debacle had actually started at number 1, more like 700. The guy in charge grabbed my attention with a rude click of his fingers and then tapped his cameraman on the shoulder to start rolling.

On came the camera's red light and I realised that I hadn't really decided on what to say, so I sat there for a few moments trying to think of something terribly funny - nothing came to my mind. Typical of Rich Harrison, I just started talking and hoped for the best.

"Well... hello there, you can call me Rich. Not because I have lots of money, but because it's my name. You know, short for Richard. So, you're probably wondering why I'm on here making a tit of myself when clearly I should be having guys throw themselves at me..." At that point I looked up at the guy in charge and added "...oh, does it matter that

I'm gay - is this even a gay thing?" I looked around a bit seeing if there was a sign somewhere while the guy in charge was waving at me and pointing to the camera. I turned back and carried on recording. "…so, if you want a good time, give me a shout – 711, like the convenience stores, only I'm not open all hours – not unless you're hot. Oh and that was my friend, Jane, who you saw just before me, unless this doesn't go out in numerical order. Anyway, she's single and I think she needs more help than me - she's still living with her mother and needs a good, hard shag."

The red light went off and so did Jane. She didn't find my last line as funny as I did, and stormed off in tears. I ran after her to apologise, but I couldn't see where she went. After a lap of the bar, I went outside to see if I could find her, pulling out my phone to call her and tell her to come back when I noticed I had a message from Dylan. I paused for a few seconds before opening it, then I did and it read "hey babe miss t hears. want u and hope its book between us. speak soon…"

My brow wrinkled up as I tried to decipher the message; clearly he'd had a few drinks and the predictive text had passed him by momentarily. I mentally reconstructed the message to understand that he missed me and hoped that it was cool between us. I didn't really know what to think – had this come a few weeks ago I would have been ecstatic about it and would have run back as fast as I could. As it stood, it had been a month since we broken up and now that I was mostly over the pain; did I want to go back for more? I thought for a while about it and left my options open by sending a pretty non-committal response, "yeah it's cool – miss you too. catch you later". We would see if anything came of it. Still I couldn't find Jane, so I got my jacket and left.

Three nights later I was still glued to the dating channel to see if my message would appear. Seriously, they should have jumped at the chance of having me on there to make their system look better; I should have been uploaded days ago.

I decided to take a well-earned break of stalking myself on the television to make a late night snack. Opening the fridge I dug around for some food that I could stuff together but all I managed to scrounge was a piece of slightly furry cheese and half a loaf of multigrain bread - or were they mouse droppings? As I was preparing my oh-so-appealing cheese sandwich, the phone rang. I snatched it up and noticed "Calan calling" flashing on the screen. I fumbled with the buttons before I managed to press the right one.

"Hi Calan" I said, perhaps with too much enthusiasm. Usually I would let it go to voicemail so I could vet a clients needs but recently I was leaping at the phone even before the first line of "Don't Cha" was sung. It appeared that in the past three months, through situations out of my control, I had managed to alienate, offend and terrify most of my current clients and a few potential new ones, too. I was officially the old fruit sitting in the market that everyone walked by and was getting worried about the cost of living. The few calls that were coming in were very welcome indeed.

Calan was not your average homosexual or average human being for that matter. Raving, debauched old freak was more the case. He enjoyed being tied up, spanked and peed on – clearly a romantic at heart. My eyes glazed over with disinterest as I listened to his order that sounded more like he was ordering a Chinese. "I want you to eat me out, followed by a good pee, with a nice pounding for afterwards." My eyes glanced across to the TV and I saw a hideous face on there; blotchy, un-cleansed and with one red line gracing the forehead; it was Jane! I yelled out suddenly "Oh my God, the chips are on fire" and hung up on him as I ran over to the couch, vaulted it with one deft movement and landed on the plump cushions, already probing the remote to turn up the volume.

"...because I really think Bros were just ahead of their time. So, you should call me if you want to meet. JANE, as in Tarzan and Jane."

I sat on the couch holding my breath as the directions came up for calling her mailbox. I couldn't look, it was like watching a scary movie just knowing the hideous monster was about to strike. And there I was: extreme close-up on my 32" flat screen. Holy sweet mother of Prada, I looked dreadful; bad lighting and sound had reduced me to one of those people you saw on late night television and felt sorry for. I didn't realise how long I'd waited until I started to speak and you'd have thought they would have edited out the gigantic pause before I started at least.

"Well...hello there, you can call me Rich. Oh, not because I have lots of money. It's my name...you know, short for Richard?..."

I closed my eyes dreading the rest of it. Thankfully it was over before I had too much time to dwell on it and up came my contact details for leaving messages. I grabbed the phone and dialled to find if I had any.

"You have no messages..."

Great stuff, I had just been inducted into the sad, lonely, wankers club.

There are many ways in which I liked to relax and enjoy myself; reading the morning paper when there isn't a single sound outside, listening to an album or two on my iPod uninterrupted, or just sitting home having a TV dinner and watching re runs of 'Sex and the City' until I fell asleep. Sitting on the kitchen floor eating dry Rice Crispies out of the box with a spoon never made it onto my list but that was how I started today.

Most of my last clients earnings had been blown on over-priced vodka tonics at some posh bar a few nights ago, the remaining shrapnel needed to see me though the rest of the week, or at least until Wednesday when I had booked a meeting with Tony bloody Tonsils out of desperation. The mere thought of him made dry-heave on my Crispies, but due to hunger, I suppressed the gag reflex and carried on eating. When did it all start going wrong? I was having such a good time and raking in cash from anyone and everyone who had a cock. Now all I got were the dried up, jizz-stained oldies who wanted to act out everything that had ever been banned.

How was it Dylan never seemed to have a lack of clients? He wasn't so different from me was he? If anything he seemed to have to turn some away, once or twice referring them to me; a kind act in retrospect, but I never got over the fact that it made me feel like a charity case. I let out a hefty sigh and finished the box of cereal, leaving my mouth tingling from the sugar overload. I scraped myself off the floor to peek into the fridge, eyeing a measly splash of milk left in the carton, barely enough to fill a tablespoon but I gulped it down all the same. Then I scraped out the last of the cheese spread from the tub with my fingers, weeded out the still-crisp lettuce from the brown curly bits and managed to find a single Lindtt chocolate that had gotten stuck to the back of the fridge. In one mouthful I munched down the lot.

My feast was interrupted by the phone ringing, which I rushed to answer in the hope that a fit, hung stud wanted to splay me for hours and fill my pockets with cash. I didn't recognise the number on the display and hesitated before answering. When I heard Dylan on the other end, I panicked and let pointless words spill from my mouth. In under a minute I had apologised, forgiven him, explained why I thought I was having a mid-life crisis, declared poverty, told him all about Tony Tonsils and even begged him to take me back – and he hadn't even told me why he was calling. I drew a breath and let him speak. He said that he wanted to meet up; he needed to talk to me. I was excited and shocked at the same time, but went along with it to see where it would lead. He seemed cool with that and said that he would wait for a text from me.

As soon as I'd hung up I frantically searched my contacts list as I needed to call someone and analyse it all. Juan sounded pleased to hear from me, almost jovial. Unbelievably and inexplicably, in the few days since I had seen him he had gotten married. He even had the audacity to use the words 'love at first sight'. Enquiring further he told me he had tied the knot to Larry who appeared to be something of a catch. His finer points ran thusly: 71 years old, sixteen stone, arthritic, diabetic, often paralytic and filthy rich. How I missed this one I'll never know. I arranged to meet him at Starbucks for all the details.

Even after allowing for him and arriving late, he still managed to be later. I was embarrassed because I only had enough money for one latte and had been drinking from the same mug since I arrived over an hour ago. Juan finally sauntered in loudly with a "Ciao darling" and plonking himself down next to me. I asked him where his new husband was and he looked at me. "I don't know" he said with a shrug and a laugh.

"I thought newlyweds went everywhere together?"

"Not in public darling – no, no, no. But his car brought me here so we are kind of here together. By the by, his chauffer is *hot*!"

I sighed quietly. "So, tell me all – this marriage thing – kinda sudden, isn't it?"

"Well, it was perfect. I was just having a spot of lunch between appointments when in wheeled this wealthy looking man..."

"Wheeled?"

"Yes darling, by his nurse. Anyway, she read him the menu, ordered for him, cut his food into pieces and then left him alone to eat it"

"I'm sorry - Nurse? Wheeled?"

"Mm-hmm. Well, she was in charge of his oxygen tank – he can't go anywhere without being attached! *Anyway -*" he said loudly, signalling for me to be quiet as I started to interrupt again. "- when I was sure she had gone, I took a seat at his table and we fell in love." Just like that. Millions of people across the globe found this one of the hardest things to accomplish yet he had mastered it in less than seven seconds. As we drank and chatted he went on to tell me that rather than chat Larry up, he simply made big, lusty eyes across the table much to the disgust of the other diners. Larry tried to say something, or possibly scream for security, but his oxygen mask had obscured his words. Juan then stuck out a Prada-clad foot and played footsies under the table. Larry smiled at the feeling of human contact, probably the first for decades other than that off his nurse - Larry then began to make big eyes back at Juan - that or he was suffocating. Larry tried to reach out and hold Juan's hand, Juan had shuddered at that and instead unzipped his top to the navel and licked his lips as if he were Rita Hayworth. Larry became transfixed with him so Juan went in for the kill. Three minutes into their chance meeting, he mouthed the words 'marry me' so that the other diners wouldn't be further put off their starters.

And as absurd as it sounds, that evening they had their first date. It sounded so romantic; Larry sat in the back seat of his Daimler while Juan wandered the aisles of Selfridges, picking out things Larry had agreed to buy him. A day later they had had their second date, just as romantic as the first, only this time Larry joined him in DeBeers and they picked out a watch together. As they left the store, Larry eyed Juan's posterior with his good eye and delight while Juan eyed his sparkly new wrist adornment with similar excitement, and soon after they had gotten married, thanks to Larry's financial assistance.

I sat there taking in the absurdity of it all, but realised that if anyone could do it, he could. Before he was able to launch into more self-adorning conversation about his love of Larry's credit limit I cut him off by blurting out "Dylan called me."

No response, he just stared at me deadpan. It was at that point I noticed that his skin looked flawless and told him so.

"It's Clarins darling, a wedding present from Lenny."

"Larry" I corrected, to which he smiled sheepishly and ushered me to continue with my story.

"So yeah, he called me – I was totally unprepared. I was cool and calm. Well, I could have been cooler. And calmer. But he called me!"

"Does he want a mercy fuck?"

"What?"

"You know – the 'I've broken up with you so let's just have one last bang and then we can move on forever' fuck."

"Gee – you know, this is the time I needed to hear something soothing and inspiring – I'm so glad I didn't call someone else!"

"I'm just being honest. Someone has to be. So, what did he want then?"

"He wants to meet and have a chat – maybe to clear the air? Why else would he want to see me? Maybe he just needed some time and is now ready to pick up where we left off!"

Juan sat stony faced.

"What?"

"Nothing!"

"Juan – I know you too well. I can tell when you're lying – you breathe!"

"All I'm saying is don't get too excited, I know you too, remember? Sad, desperate and willing to fling yourself into the arms of anyone who should look at you for fear of being left on the shelf"

"Shall I just get you a big stick to hit me with – it might be quicker?"

"Sweetie – be real. You don't get where I am today without having a good grasp on reality"

"Oh really, and tell me again about Larry?" I retorted in anger.

Our conversation was interrupted by Juan's phone. It was the chauffer.

"No, no – I'm coming now Roberto – two minutes. Oh, Roberto, that seatbelt is still funny; you'll have to have a little fiddle with it for me." He made his excuses and left me where I started – sitting alone in Starbucks and with a million thoughts of Dylan racing through my head.

I knew I shouldn't have but I couldn't resist texting Dylan to agree to meeting up with him. The reality was I had written another small essay. He didn't text back that evening until very late when I was on the phone to my old friend, Jade, who had moved to Amsterdam. Dylan had replied and was seeing if I could meet for some dinner on Monday night. It had been such a long time since I had seen a message from him in my inbox as I had deleted all the others to resist the temptation to keep going back to them. Well, when I say I deleted them, Juan had deleted several and Jacqui threatened to insert the phone in me if I didn't delete the rest. It felt good to see his name there again and for a few moments, I was back to where it all began.

That night in bed I wasn't able to sleep very much. It was a warm night and I just rolled around, getting tangled in the sheets and willing myself to fall asleep. I eventually drifted off sometime after four.

Brunch the next day was courtesy of Jacqui and Debs. Debs' flat was being repainted, and the scent of new paint and wood stain was oddly comforting. Jacqui had insisted on cooking for us, and while she busied herself in Debs' kitchen, Debs and I sat outside soaking up the sun.

Soon, Jacqui brought out some fabulous eggs made with spinach and cheese and I greedily shovelled the food into my hungry tummy, followed closely by a home-brewed espresso. Minutes later I was ready for another helping, and sat delighted at the table while Jacqui served up seconds and Debs poured more of the thick black coffee.

We talked about loads of stuff from Dannii Minogue to Debs' period pains that had gotten so bad she was actually scared to be around people for fear of battering them with any nearby heavy object. And of course we talked about Dylan. They were both very sweet and encouraging – but like Juan, they warned me not to get too excited.

"Don't kiss him" offered Jacqui.

"Don't FUCK him!" added Debs.

"Don't listen to her – she's blobbing. But really Rich, be careful. By all means, meet him and enjoy him for all it's worth, but be aware that he may just want to finalise it in his mind. It might be his way of closure.

"Yeah, I hear you, but I just can't help feel that this is a rekindling! I have such a strong feeling that he is going to take me back and it's all going to be like it was before - without all of my nuttiness of course."

My statement was met with raised eyebrows and silence. Debs reassured me that if it did all go tits up; they would be waiting for me with another fat bottle of Vodka to soften the blow. Bless them.

As I left them later that morning, I thought long and hard about what they had told me. I knew deep down in the back of my mind they were probably right and I should really prepare a soft landing for myself, but as much as I knew this, I couldn't shake this good feeling I had. After all these months apart, Dylan didn't need to meet up with me to finalise a break-up – surely not. I headed home with wonderful thoughts in my head.

As Keane blasted away on my iPod, I sat on the bus gazing out into the bustle of the streets, half thinking about Dylan and half dreaming about finally being content. It was then that I had the feeling someone was watching me. I glanced up and sure enough, a fairly handsome looking man was trying to catch my eye. If there's one thing I hated it was being stared at so I gave him a sharp look, and then returned to my daydreaming through the window. However, I still had the feeling his eyes were on me. He wasn't stunning, but he wasn't ugly either. He was average bordering hot, maybe forty two, forty three? Dressed ok;

brown suede jacket, light coloured trousers....oh, and loafers with no socks, ew.

Now that I had to concentrate on daydreaming; I sat up again and looked across to him. He was still looking. I raised my eyebrows slightly – I didn't want to confront him as the bus was quite busy, so I hoped that with a curt nod of my head he would get the idea that I was irritated and to leave me alone. As I left the bus at Kings Cross Station, so did he. Trying not to look alarmed I quickened my pace to a brisk walk; some would say mince. Every few steps, I would try to glance over my shoulder to see if he was following me - he was. As I neared a newspaper kiosk I slowed down, thankful of the few people bustling around and I busied myself with a magazine, trying to think what I should do when he came and stood right next to me. I clammed up until he reached out a hand to grab me, causing me to drop my magazine and walk off speedily. I knew he was still walking along behind me though; I could feel his eyes burning small holes into the back of my jacket, so I glanced over my shoulder again and confirmed my suspicion. Without thinking I swung into a phone box that was on the corner of the street and firmly pulled the door close behind me. I picked up the receiver and didn't know what to do – I was dumbfounded – I hadn't been in a public phone box since I was at school – by today's day and age, hadn't mobile phones eradicated any need for them? However long it had been, it was obviously a great deal longer than I thought as I was now staring at a computerised monitor offering me the internet and a myriad of other options. Now he was knocking on the window outside, making me shriek in response. I got out my mobile and aimed it at him.

"I've seen your face - I have taken a picture of you and I'm going to send it to the police!" I screamed. He looked confused, but carried on knocking. "I mean it; I will send it to them right now, so fuck off!" Through the window he just laughed at me while I put my hands over the glass in an attempt to obscure him but he just picked another window to peer through, winking again. He signalled for me to open the door. Reluctantly I pulled it open a jar, just enough to hear what he was saying. "What do you want – I have no money and you'd hate my iPod – really, sometimes even I skip songs!"

"I think I've seen you on the telly!" I relaxed a little; thinking he thought I was famous, but then remembered it was probably the dating channel.

"M-maybe – maybe you have. Why?"

"Oh good – I thought it was you. I didn't get your box number on that date show thing and I wanted to message you. I couldn't believe it when I saw you on the bus. You're really handsome in real life – much better than on the telly!"

I took this more as a compliment than an insult and opened the door fully. We chatted for a minute or two and I calmed down when he offered to take me for a drink. He wasn't my type really, we didn't have anything in common so we did what was only natural – I blew him in the bar toilet and he gave me forty quid. The rest of the afternoon was highly average in comparison – the highlight was me being nice and comfy on my sofa, dozing off to a DVD.

Early Monday morning, under my duvet.

It's official. I just had the best dream of my life; Dylan and I were standing in line in Sainsbury's, when all of a sudden Dale Winton came up and told us that we were on Celebrity Supermarket Sweep and that the first prize would be a marriage and honeymoon in French Guiana. As most dreams go, it got stranger and stranger, where instead of having to pull groceries into our trolleys, they were miniature heads. Well, Dale told us we had won and the next thing we knew, were standing on a beach, Dylan picking me up in his arms and kissing me. It was the most realistic sensation I have ever had in a dream, so much so, that when I awoke, I was entwined with my pillow and sheets; tongue out and licking the pillowcase. What a great start to a Monday, so much so that I felt like treating myself today. Enough with the barbers – I was going to the swankiest hairdresser I could find and then buy some new clothes to reward myself.

An hour and a half later saw me showered, dressed and out the front door of my flat. I walked down the high road to the station; already nervous about tonight's meeting with Dylan. I couldn't help but over-analyse things like this, and although it was almost ten hours until I saw him, I was thinking through all the possibilities of what would happen. I caught the tube to Leicester Square and walked to my hair appointment from there. I'd never really been big on hairdressers; mainly due to the fact that I wasn't that comfortable paying fifty quid for a mediocre haircut that took two hours. I'd much rather go to an in-and-out business where they would cut your hair and keep the conversation to the bare minimum. Arriving at the door of the hairdressers, I looked up. In front of me were two imposing, old Moroccan doors, intricately carved and set with gigantic handles. Each was twice my height and several widths of me wide. Fooled by the look of these works of art I used all my body weight and leant into them, giving them a hard shove, finding that they actually opened with unexpected ease and banged ferociously against their jambs. Every head in the hairdressers turned to face me, even the ones half-submerged into sinks. Inside was pure hubbub and noise, very daunting; people running around all over the place, armed with combs, straighteners and random hair-manipulating tools. The main part of the studio was set up with cosy little leather couches and armchairs, each one on a raised platform facing an old fashioned, gilt framed mirror on a pedestal. Every seat was occupied with a client; each one having their hair viciously attacked by a stylist. Towards the back of the establishment was a gigantic brass water trough etched with a further intricate design, and surrounded by tilting chairs, obviously used for hair washing.

"Good morning sir" said a voice to my left. I turned around and nearly jumped out of my skin. "Mother fuck!!" I exclaimed obviously offending the owner of the voice. In front of me, behind a wooden counter was the receptionist. I wasn't sure if there was an accident, but she seemed to have had half her hair hacked away, dyed a hideous colour, then piled up on top of her head and affixed with a few industrial-sized clamps.

"Oh...uh...sorry" I gushed "only that you scared me...I was thinking about something else". Truth is, I was thinking about something else – I was thinking how to back out of the hairdressers without them noticing. Too late, she kept talking.

"Can I have you name please?"

"Uhhh...it's Rich" I said, half distracted from the people around me.

"Come with me please" she smiled, her hair leading the way. She sat me on one of the raised comfortable chairs and I looked around feeling terribly conspicuous in my bland attire. Around me were sat bright, young things, wearing their statements to the world through their clothing, hairstyles and random piercings. The guy seated on my left was stunning; tall, pitch black hair, high cheekbones and a lean, muscled body hidden under a ripped, tight, horizontal striped t-shirt. He glanced up at me briefly and looked straight back down at his magazine. Nice, I had just gotten a tenth-of-a-second assessment and clearly I had failed. This was not my sort of place at all – maybe I should've just left.

"Rich? Hey, I'm Terri." I looked around and stood before me now was another fashion icon, decked out in seventies glam, complete with poker straight, blonde hair.

"Oh…hello" I ventured, trying not to sound too much like a private school boy. "And what have you come as?"

After a minute's silence, she spoke to my reflection, rather than me. "What are we doing today" she asked, already messing around with my hair – pulling at it, making it stand on end, flattening it against my forehead - each style making it look more ridiculous than the last.

"Um…oh…well I just wanted to go a little shorter – it's a bit scruffy and…"

"Oh…scruffy is so hot right now" she interjected as if I should have known.

"Okay…well let's keep it scruffy, but maybe a bit shorter in places" I suggested, hoping that I hadn't offended anyone around me.

"Nice…let's get you washed".

As she sat me down at the basin, the guy who had been sitting next to me was also led over, taking the seat next to mine. Even his stylist was cute – all I had to flirt with was a younger version of Blondie. While I was on my third condition (was my hair that bad?), I realised what I'd been missing all those years at the barbers: they never gave me a head massage, the closest they ever came to that was when the comb got stuck in my knots and they had to yank it free. I slinked into my chair, letting out a contented sigh. Unfortunately, due to the fact that I had to express satisfaction on command by my very job, it was quite an orgasmic sigh and terribly loud. My eyes darted open and I noticed everyone was looking at me.

"Oh…uh…sorry" I said sheepishly and flashed Terri a smile. I was led back to the chair, as was the guy next to me, and while Terri was busy adjusting my cape, his stylist had already started working him over. They were both blatantly making eyes to each other in the mirror; I had a DVD that started out that way before the client was bent over the basin and pounded by the randy hairdresser. Shit, I was getting hard under my cape. Terri adjusted the chair height and began to style my hair again with her hands. Through force of habit she started her routine of chit chat and asked me what it was like outside, or if I was a lunch break. I gave her some simple responses while I tried to watch the guys to my left from the corner of my eye without going blind. I wasn't really paying attention to the next question she asked, so without thinking I answered "I'm a male escort..."

She stopped halfway through a cut with her scissors; the hairdresser and guy next to me both look over, staring. I sat upright in my chair, staring straight ahead at my reflection in the mirror.

"Oh...my...God" started Terri, "that's fucking awesome".

And in four words I had gone from geek to God. For the next forty minutes, the four of us were madly laughing and chatting and sharing stories. It turned out the customer next to me had done a brief stint in escorting before his modelling took off, and we were able to share some horror stories of clients gone wrong. Naturally, I had the best stories; a client who cried when I wouldn't go home with him, hiding in another's wardrobe when his wife came home, having to lie there while someone worshipped my feet. Really, I was quite proud that my life could be viewed as such good entertainment.

As I walked outside with my hot new haircut (a few colours thrown in for free), I was thinking about the other client in the hairdressers. He had moved on to the next act in his performance, having scored a lucrative deal with Vans. Maybe this was why my clients were all drying up – had I stayed beyond my curtain call? I wondered if Dylan was thinking along the same sort of lines. Maybe I could bring it up with him. It wasn't like I really had anyone in the industry to talk to about it, well, there was Juan but he never really saw it as business, more of a lifestyle. He would never turn his back on his audience - he was the Madonna of the gigolo world. I had managed most of the day without dwelling too much on Dylan, but now he was all I could think of. My hands had become clammy just at the thought of his name, I really liked him, more than liked him. I was just petrified of meeting up with him and having the few little hopes that I had built up dashed away. Even though I was being as pragmatic as I could, I was really only prepared for our date to go one way – mine. Then it hit me like a fat kid wearing boxing gloves; I was in love! It suddenly occurred to me of what my issue has been all this time. Not stupid teenage or twenty-something love - this was it, the real thing.

Stopping suddenly in the middle of the high street, I let this thought wash over me. Love – yeah, that was it. I had been struck by cupid's arrow! It wasn't jealousy I felt when I thought about him working – it was anger. I didn't want anyone else to touch him, he was supposed to be mine, all mine.

By the time I had finished my epiphany, I practically ran up the high street for the train, excited to get ready and come back out to meet him. Tonight I would put my heart on the line and tell him how it was - best case scenario being we would marry in a fortnight with some fabulous orchestra playing behind us, worse case being eating myself to death by full submersion in a vat of chocolate sauce. Either way, feeling all torn up inside would be over soon enough.

Hot New Indian Restaurant, Brick Lane.

To put it simply, I looked hot. I had never looked this good, dressed in a designer brown pinstripe suit, fitted shirt and my new snakeskin shoes. I looked the part so much that even I would have slept with me if I could have. I paced up and down in front of the restaurant and twice went inside to make sure I hadn't missed him. Ten minutes later as I started to worry, I saw him coming up the street and when he reached me, all I could do was stare into his beautiful eyes, one of which winked at me.

"Hey!" he smiled, planting a kiss on my forehead in a hurried greeting.

"Oh…hi…" I stammered, not really knowing if I was excited or insulted.

"Yes…and it's good to see you too" I half bowed trying to work out what the hell I was doing. He paused for a moment and then sweetly gestured me into the restaurant.

The foyer was dimly lit and gorgeous; soft Indian music played in the background and sweet incense curled up in billows around us, scenting the air. All around were carved statues and opulent paintings covering the rich, dark wooden walls, and toward the centre of the foyer was an attractive pool of gently bubbling water, lit from below and strewn with fresh lilies. The waiter led us to the back of the restaurant to a table which faced out onto a pretty little courtyard. Still a few months too cold to venture outside but it made me feel a little like I was on holiday.

"How are…"
"What's the…"

We both started our sentences together, and then stopped, looking at each other to continue. It was like a first date all over again and I got a little rush of excitement.

"Sorry, carry on" I said.

"It's okay, I was just going to ask how you were" Dylan smiled at me, looking genuinely interested in my response.

"Great...yup...very cool thanks – and you?" I responded. Nice one Rich, you're the master of dialogue, I thought to myself.

"Well, yeah, I'm good thanks. Kinda strange over the past few weeks though, a lot has been going on with me. But I wanted us to meet up to talk through some things." As he kept talking I began to worry. He was happy where he was – no, maybe he was going to get back together with that dreadful old man he was with – or worse, Mark. Why didn't he want me? "We may as well just get this out in the open and then we can enjoy our dinner" he said without looking me in the eye "I have decided to go travelling." The words came crashing through my thoughts and hit me in the face. I stopped thinking and stared at him, his face wrought with concern, waiting for my response. I swallowed hard not knowing what I was to say.

"Well I think that's a stellar idea, a little holiday will do you the world of good. I hear that Derbyshire isn't all that bad; I mean they're a bit weird there, but apparently they have some good cheese."

"No, Rich, I was thinking a little further than that. I've got savings, ideally I was planning to get a house or something but this could be the only chance I have to do this. I'm probably going to spend some time in Australia before...." And I started to zone out. I sat there for literally minutes, unable to comprehend what I had just heard. Every time I opened my mouth to reply, nothing came out so I snapped it closed. As soon as I had, I opened it to speak again, but then snapped it shut. I looked like a dying haddock. His words then snapped me out of my trance.

"....and after a year or so I'll have done most of Asia, then I guess if there's any cash left, see where else I can go to. I know that's quite a big thing to come out with. But I've been thinking about it for a while now."

I should have kept calm and composed, but I couldn't help it. Without thinking I barked my response, probably a little too loudly.

"Are you *insane*?! Do you know what types of diseases you could catch being a *gigolo* in those places?" As soon as I'd said this, the conversation among the other diners fell to a hush. "It's ok" I declared standing up, addressing the room. "I'm an actor and I'm just practising my lines. Please carry on with your meals." As I sat back down, he was looking angry.

"Jesus Rich, what are you doing? I have seriously thought this through, you know. I am tired of doing this, I'm almost 30! I need to change my life I'm starting with me. No more escorting, no more sleeping around. This is perfect for me; you know how much I love to travel – there's an entire world out there just waiting for me!"

"I think I'll have a Jalfrezi" I said rather pointlessly.

He looked at me like I was mental. I had just confirmed his suspicions.

"Did you listen to what I just said? You have to talk to me – I'm not here just to amuse myself." He looked angry for a second but his face softened and he carried on. "I wanted to bring you here because…"

"Yes. Yes I heard you Dylan. Loudly. Clearly. I heard you."

Another strange look. "Good, because I want to know…"

"Is a Jalfrezi hot?" I asked as I waved my arm around to attract the waiter's attention to save me from this conversation. Dylan looked totally stunned and couldn't manage to spit any more words out for the moment, so we sat in near silence until the waiter came and took our order for drinks and food. At times, he tried to catch my eye, but as soon as he did I would force myself to look at something else. Inside I was still angry and upset but on the outside I was trying to look like I wasn't bothered. I don't think I was doing a great job.

"Are you ok?"

"Fine. Totally fine, fine, fine. So, Austria, that's nice"

"Australia. Rich, I know you're upset, but I really do need to talk to you about this – if you can just let me tell you…"

Just then it struck me that he wasn't going travelling. What an idiot I was – silly Rich. He had met someone, a tall, spunky Australian, probably online, and they had fallen in love. I looked up at him while he was still in mid conversation, but I wasn't listening. My eyes were filled with fear and resentment.

"You're gonna be Bruce's Sheila! Strewth! "

Why the hell did I just say that? Dylan now looked positively petrified. Well, if he was getting loved up, then I was going to as well. Where was that waiter? I decided to make him jealous and flirt my socks off. As the skinny waiter came with our drinks, I whipped my napkin from my legs onto the floor and called out for his assistance.

"Sorry, so sorry. My napkin has slipped – would you be a darl and get it for me?"

With this, I gestured to my thrusting groin as if I were Rik Mayall. The waiter who was barely older than fifteen scurried away as quickly as he arrived.

"Rich – what are you doing?"

"Nothing. It's not my fault if people find me irresistible is it?"

"Who – him? He's a child! And you're going to get us thrown out!" he said, sounding alarmed.

"Oh piffle. I'm just enjoying myself, and I can't help it if I'm drunk". As soon as I'd said that I realised I hadn't even touched my beer, so thought it best to act on impulse and gulp it down in one. With watery eyes, I looked over to Dylan who was staring at the table. Soon enough, the waiter appeared, practically threw the food at us and left before I could further accost him. I looked back to Dylan who was pushing his food around the plate, not really interested in actually eating it and I sat muttering to myself. Whenever the waiter neared our table to serve the nearby guests, he quickened his pace and the returned to normal speed once he had cleared us.

"Another beer please, hon!" I called out.

I think the beer was starting to get to me though, I was feeling warm. Then I realised that my Sag Aloo was sliding off my spoon onto my stomach and lap. "Oh, bugger". I looked up at Dylan who was mortified. Typical of me really; thinking back to all the daft things I had done when we were together, nothing was more cringe worthy than tonight. Surely I had sealed my fate. If Dylan was even half tempted to rekindle what we had I had surely blown it.

"So, who is he then?" This caused Dylan to put his fork down and look up at me. God, he was so handsome. And I was so jealous.

"Who? What are you on about?"

"Broo-ooce" I said with silly rolling eyes and a shake of my head.

"You know Rich, sometimes you're insufferable!"

I paused for a moment before thanking him for what I thought was a compliment. After he told me what it meant, I was most offended. "Oh, I am, am I?!"

"If you ever stop to think about someone else other than you, you might realise that perhaps people aren't here to be against you all the time. It's not always Rich versus the world you know" His voice was slightly raised, but he was being careful enough not to shout. I was a little frightened; I had never seen him like this before. "Give a guy a break will you" he continued "I mean think back to all the mad stuff you did when we were dating; hiding in plants, texting me on the hour every hour, going through my phone!"

I tried to intercept, but realised I only needed to burp and made myself suppress it.

"In fact, there aren't many guys who would have tolerated you for very long, you know?"

Now I *was* offended. Before I could stand up for myself though, Dylan reached out his hand. Thinking he was going to hit me I flinched and shut my eyes. I opened them when I felt his warm hand on mine. His voice had softened again and he was looking me dead in the eye.

"But I did tolerate you and I'm glad I did. You're something very special. Ok, slightly mental and probably imbalanced, but still special."

I opened my mouth to speak, but he shook his head.

"No, don't say anything – if I know you by now, you'll probably say something stupid and endearing. I have to say this to you before you get all bent out of shape. And you're going to listen to me, ok?" I nodded.

"Right – since we met, I have had you on my mind constantly! You're a bumbling twit at times, but you have such a way about you, I know that everything you do is out of love and consideration. I know that it all goes wrong for you when you try to do well, and the way you try to cover it all up with an even bigger mess is wonderful. I can see into your heart and I know that you're a special person. Just like I know you see into my heart. I love you Rich. I never thought I'd say this, but what we had was love at first sight. At times you freaked me out, and it's taken this long for me to realise that we should be together. I'm really sorry that it's taken me this long to work through it all, but I did need time to understand everything"

"But why are you fucking off to Austria then?"

"Australia. Look at me – I'm a bloody male escort – how can I ever look myself in the eye and be proud of myself. This isn't me, the sex, the waiting around, the secrecy – I need to find some normality. I need someone special in my life, and up until I met you I hadn't found him. I'm tired of looking Rich."

At that moment, I let all my barriers down and try one last time "I can be that person. I can be the thing you need. If you only would reconsider about this trip – stay with me, we can give it another go? Can't we?"

"You don't understand."

"I do! I do understand. Please give me a chance!" I pleaded.

"No you don't understand Rich, really. I want you to come travelling with me. Let's do it together."

Juan's flat, Knightsbridge.

Juan didn't invite me over often but since I was last here the place had been totally redecorated. I thought it looked fine before, but since then he had really polished the place up. The living room was gorgeous, lined by two dark leather modular sofas. Along the centre of the room between them ran a long heavy-looking glass table dotted with art literature, political magazines and copies of *Heat*. This led to the garden area which seemed to also have been made over with its newly manicured lawn and patio area. Jacqui and Debs sat alongside me, and I could tell they were as equally impressed as I was.

I had called Juan and the girl's minutes after my dinner ended (as I was walking my curry-stained self back to the underground) and told them I needed to see them. Juan suggested his place and he even invited the girls around.

"There's no sense in me not making an effort with your other friends Rich, even if they are slug rubbers." I was lost. "Slug rubbers! Rug Munchers. Carpet Lickers...*lesbians*". He whispered the last word as if it were the highest form of insult – funny really, given the trail of verbal insults he had just fired off. He really had no clue about any other life outside of his admittedly fabulous little world.

"They're not lesbians Juan" I said, sighing.

However, I did appreciate his gesture of having the girls over, and here we all were. I had never thought my friends would gel, and to be honest I was a little nervous that they wouldn't even like each other, especially Debs and Juan; two strong personalities in one small suburb of Greater

London does not usually make a good mix. We sat in silence while he banged around in the kitchen, before mincing into the room with a tray of mini Lebanese pizzas and other M&S-inspired canapés.

"I'm impressed – I didn't think you were so…homely. Homo yes, but homely, no" I chuckled.

"I know, isn't it fabulous! I did it all myself!

"Really – that's great!"

"Mm-hmm, I just pointed to it in a magazine and some fabulous people came and made it happen!"

Jacqui offered a polite giggle to the room, but I knew Juan was being deadly serious.

We chatted about such pleasantries as home furnishings, Big Brother and Juan's recent divorce. Apparently three weeks was the most Juan could last being tied to one man. In fact, that's what caused the divorce. Juan had suggested that he and Larry indulge in a little bit of bedroom fun as simply spending all of Larry's money had now bored him. To spice things up, he tied Larry's hands together and above his head to the bedpost, but Larry had a minor fit of panic and lost control of his fluids, and his solids. This proved too much for Juan and his £300 Christian La Croix bed linen, and a divorce was sought along with a hefty settlement which had obviously paid for his recent home makeover. Juan explained that Larry said some nasty things about him as they were breaking up, so he justified his payout as deformation of character, but we really knew it was just defecation on bedding.

The mini pizzas were gone within minutes and the conversation soon swung round to my night with Dylan. I was aching, literally aching to blurt it all out, but I could feel their disapproval already and was frightened to tell them.

"Nice? Just nice?" squeaked Jacqui. I nodded as I played with my serviette.

"Did you fuck him, sweetie?" asked Juan, dabbing at his mouth. Sensing the girls' glares he waved them off. "It's ok if you did – the mercy fuck, like we spoke about." He turned to face the girls. "Mercy fuck" he said again, pointing to me and nodding.

I told them all that I hadn't and that it was just a really good night. I left out the part about the sexual harassment of the underage waiter and the paranoia that had consumed me for most of the night. But I knew they weren't buying it. Debs had a scary way of knowing when I wasn't telling all so I put my serviette down.

"Ok, we might need a drink for what I'm about to tell you guys". Before Juan was able to stand, Debs had pulled a bottle of vodka from her bag.

"Travelling? You! Come off it Rich, you need a map to get around the supermarket!" Jacqui laughed in my face when I told her. I felt sheepish and embarrassed.

"No no, Dylan has planned it all actually – he says it's going to be great"

"Oh, Dylan, I knew it!" snapped Debs.

"No, not just because of Dylan" I said defensively. "This is something I would like to do also. I do have a brain thank you." This was met with silence.

"Well you can't. There's no way you can go. Absurd!" Debs looked angry and panicked as she spoke and looked at me for confirmation that I agreed.

"He can go if he wants – like a little holiday. I'll come with you sweetie!" added Juan, not helping matters at all.

"No. No he can't. He has a life here. And friends. And commitments. And family, it's impossible – I hope you told Dylan to stick this bloody pipe dream up…up his bloody pipe!"

Jacqui sat quietly, swigging at the bottle of vodka, just making faces that she agreed with Debs. I knew it was going to be hard for them to comprehend, but I was thinking about going with him as soon as he mentioned it to me. I was so touched by everything he had said to me last night – I had been swept off my feet, just like I always had wanted. My eyes glazed over for a second and I thought about him. I tried to reassure them all, but might have dug my hole a little deeper.

"It's only a year!" I said.

Debs then went into overdrive "Oh my God" she said, snapping me out of my day dream. "*Only* a year. Well, *that's* fine then, why didn't you say!!? You can't *seriously* be going?!"

I didn't know how to react. I was angry, defiant but also sad and a bit exposed. A pregnant pause was all Debs needed to fuel herself. "You *are*, aren't you? How can you be so irresponsible? It's not like you're going to Malaga for the weekend, you're going to away for 365 days, or more, who knows? You hardly even know him, who the fuck is this guy to come in, tell you to pack up your life and fuck off round the fucking world for a fucking year. He crushed you a few months ago and now you're going to follow him around the world. You're not even sure if he fucking loves you."

The last comment got my hackles up and I bit back.

"God Debs, what is your problem? This is a one in a lifetime opportunity for me. Have some faith in people. Not everyone has a fucked up view of love like you do." Even as it came out of my mouth, I regretted saying it.

Jacqui snorted into her drink and Juan simply stared at me. Debs stood up with a start and stormed off, however, as I was sitting near the hall door, she made her exit into the garden though she didn't get too far as she found her dramatic exit blocked by a rather large pink hydrangea and a balcony box of rosemary.

I got up and rushed out after her, Juan and Jacqui quietly debating whether or not to follow or to leave well enough alone. Juan had never heard of the latter, so after a few seconds hesitation, he came out behind me.

"Debs, that was way out of line – I'm so sorry" I called out as I walked outside. The smell of the garden temporarily distracted me from the situation I now found myself in, and I couldn't help but gain a little more respect for Juan's tastes.

Debs turned around and she was crying. God, I'd never made anyone cry in my life, I'd tried to on numerous occasions though, the most noteworthy of which was one of my old work colleagues who thought she could boss me around because she was older than me. After she had blamed me for one of her usual fuck-ups I let her have it, cursing and ranting only to watch her casually turn around halfway through to continue typing at her keyboard. Apparently I wasn't as intimidating as I thought I was (perhaps people in fawn trousers and cashmere sweaters were immune to intimidation). Here was Debs in front of me, her stay-fast mascara doing anything but its job.

I tried to look as remorseful as I could. On top of everything else I couldn't deal with my friend not talking to me.

"God Rich – don't you see? You're my best friend – we've been through so much together and…well, how am I supposed to do this without you?" she sobbed. I had never seen hers at a moment of weakness, and to be honest – it was one of the most distressing things I'd experienced.

I pulled her in for a hug which she initially resisted, then fell into me, sobbing harder. I was completely out of my depth, so I hoped that I would be able to articulate myself well enough in the situation.

"Debs…I'm always going to be here for you as a friend, but this is something for me in my life. I need change; I need to experience something…else. For so long I have been bouncing around, not really knowing what I wanted, even this whole escort thing has pretty much gone tits up. I know that you worry for me, but I don't want you to. I'm going to be fine. I know that you don't really think much of Dylan, but I only tell you the worst things when I need your support." She looked up into my eyes and smiled weakly.

"I don't know what my future holds" I continued "but I do know that no matter what happens with Dylan, this is such an exciting opportunity. Even if it goes pear-shaped with him, I will have had all these amazing places to explore. I need you to be happy for my decision and to realise that I've thought about it properly. I'm going Debs. If I hate it that much, I'll come home. It's really not that bad."

Debs pulled herself to arms length, holding my face in her hands, and she sighed. "Just make sure you don't marry a fucking Aussie and stay there; and if you do, make sure he has a couple of brothers so Jaqs and I can come and live there too."

Debs and I walked hand in hand back into Juan's living room. After the travelling issue was dealt with, we continued long into the night with Juan feeding us more Champagne and wine. Just as I thought that my girls and Juan were becoming steadfast friends who would look after each other in my absence, Juan pointed at Jacqui and said in a concerned voice, "It looks like Jacqui has had too much to drink and I think she's going to…*oh my God*" he screamed "that's my new fucking sofa!". Perhaps this new friendship group would need a little more time to gel.

Two months later - Mash Bar, Portland Street.

As I came out of the toilets and stood on the threshold of the crowded restaurant, I looked over at my friends and the few members of my family who had turned up for my fabulous leaving party. I hadn't expected my parents to come at all but it seemed that this was too big a thing for them to stay away from - I mean, I was still their son no matter who I dated. I could tell they didn't look comfortable though; Juan was sitting next to my mother, oblivious to her awkwardness as he was reeling off a list of things she could try to rekindle her sex life with my father, while my father stood steadfastly at the back of the room, his back never leaving the wall behind him.

By now, most of my guests were in a drunken state of revelry, myself included. I decided to stand there for a few minutes by the canapés to look from an outsider's point of view.

Since I had agreed to go travelling with Dylan, everything had happened so fast – too fast, in fact. Thankfully, he was able to sort out the visas and other necessary paperwork which actually wasn't as bad as I thought it would be, and while he did all the other important things like flights, vaccines and the first few nights of accommodation, I was concentrating more on the important items like shopping for shorts, toiletries and gorgeous luggage.

A leaving party also meant presents and I had received a few good ones. Among the obvious joke gifts which included a mini vibrator and sachets of lube, Juan's gift was by far the most amazing. In fact, he had given the present to me the day I had told them all I was going. After Debs and Jacqui had passed out at his place, he had taken me into the kitchen and showed me a side of himself I don't think I had ever seen before. We sat at his beautiful Italian marble breakfast bar and for a few minutes he seemed to take off the image of him that I had known like it were an old coat or something. Underneath was the real Juan who proceeded to tell me how much he valued my friendship over the last few years, and that even though he made out he was the cat's pyjamas, he really didn't have many true friends as 'all whores were selfish fucks'.

As he began to pour out some of his heart, he handed me an envelope. I was numb – I didn't know how to act around this new Juan. He urged me to open it, and inside was a cheque made out to me for £20,000. I had almost fallen off my chair when I saw it and told him there was no way I could take it, even though I had already mentally spent a few hundred quid within seconds of opening it.

"Shut up Rich" he said. "I want you to have this and enjoy your travels. You bloody deserve this. And anyway, Larry was very generous to me in the divorce".

"He was?"

"Well, ish. His signature was *so* easy to forge! But he would have wanted me to have taken it and I want you to take it now. Enjoy it. And bring me a nice present back, something by Gucci! Hey, I'll probably meet up with you in Japan later in the year, yeah? Whores do Tokyo!"

I was completely stunned. I had a couple of thousand pounds still left in my savings from long ago but not nearly enough to really enjoy travelling with. I had initially intended to get some work out in Australia and pay my way as I went. But this gift was certainly going to ensure that both Dylan and I were going to have a great time. I hugged Juan so hard that I could have snapped him into pieces. I liked the new him, he was so…nice. It didn't last long though, for as soon as I released my grip he said that I had put on weight and I ought to shed a few stone before going.

In the past couple of weeks, the girls had finally lightened up and were as excited as I was about this trip. We had all made plans for them so come and meet up with us across the globe somewhere, it was all very exciting. Meanwhile, they and Juan were becoming closer, and I was able to hang out with the three of them without feeling concerned for any of their safety.

I grabbed a bottle of wine and took myself off to a table for some quiet time to take it all in. How had I gotten here? When I thought back to how I used to sit at that checkout for years, just watching as other people lived their lives, it was incredible for me to think that here I was, living my own life – I'd had a pretty good one so far and it wasn't showing any signs of slowing.

To say I was lucky was an understatement. I had the best friends anyone could ever ask for. I had to chuckle to myself watching Jacqui and Dylan having a vodka shot contest at the bar while Juan and Debs were both flirting with a cute waiter nearby.

There was absolutely no doubt at all I was going to miss everyone so much, but I was so excited for the next adventure. Dylan and I are going to start in Australia and spend a couple of months travelling up the East Coast. I had bought so many travel guides and had spent hours reading them. Well, Dylan read them and I looked at the pictures. After Australia, New Zealand, then India, Vietnam, Burma, China and Japan – so many places, and a few I hadn't even thought of visiting.

Even shopping for things was fun; a mosquito net, tents, sleeping bags, was this real? Was I really going to do all these fabulous things that I thought only other people got to do. Everyone joked about how I wouldn't actually make it out of Terminal 4, and I had to agree I was having my own doubts. But with Dylan by my side, it could only be amazing.

As I swigged from my Riesling and looked at my friends, I felt the first pangs of separation in my gut, even though they were only a few feet away. The people here tonight to wish me well, to drink with me and cry with me weren't just run of the mill friends; each of them had contributed something special to my life. But I knew that this wasn't the end of it all, no way. I would be bombarding them with daily emails and webcam diaries, posting things back that we couldn't carry with us, and relying on them for updates on all my favourite reality shows. Hell, it was almost as if they were coming with us.

As I was about to move on with my life and start a new adventure, I wondered what I would be missing. I liked my routine and wondered if I could cope without it. I knew for one thing that I wasn't going to miss the job I was giving up. I gulped down some more wine and thought about my friends? How would I cope if it were them leaving? Up until now I had always been the one waving off close friends at the airport; a snivelling mess as I walked down to catch the Piccadilly Line back into the city.

It was certainly fair to say that my emotions this past month had been all over the place, but my decision had been made. I saw Dylan across the room – he caught my eye, raised a shot glass and mouthed that he loved me. I knew I was making the right choice and that however bad I felt for leaving my friends behind, I was doing the right thing. I owed a lot of my strength to Dylan. Now that we had both decided to leave our escorting days behind us, the insanity I had suffered from was gone…well, lessened. Unlike most couples who would screw each other and then sit in silence watching Big Brother, we were avidly looking up places to travel to, reading about culture, bars, beaches – then we'd screw.

Truth be told, I didn't know where my life was going – all I knew was that I was finally letting go of my hang-ups and issues and surrendering myself to what life had to offer.

I took a deep breath and headed back to Dylan and the party. My head was heavy with too much wine, and I hooked an arm around his shoulder. He kissed me on the cheek. "Hey" yelled Debs. "Don't hog him you greedy bastard, your taking him for yourself already, let us have a go too" and with that she barged her way over to me to plant a kiss on my cheek, smearing me with lurid, pink lipstick. She was quickly followed by Jacqui who kissed me on the other side leaving a smudgy red patch on my other cheek. Then Juan sauntered over and kissed me on the forehead leaving an imprint of his pucker in lip gloss.

I knew that Rich Harrison was going to be alright – and all the sad, lonely gits in London with hairy balls, halitosis and depraved fetishes would have to find someone else to bribe for freaky sexual favours. I had hung up my gigolo hat and had no intention of putting back on.